GLIMPSES
THROUGH
THE MIRROR

GLIMPSES THROUGH
THE MIRROR

·····································

THE COLLECTED
PEN POINT
COLUMNS

·····································

JIM CAMPBELL

To Bill o'Susan

Jim Campbell

BPS
books

Toronto and New York

Published by
BPS Books
Toronto, Canada
www.bpsbooks.com
A division of Bastian Publishing Services Ltd.
www.bastianpubserv.com

ISBN 978-1-927483-25-1

Cataloguing-in-Publication Data available from
Library and Archives Canada.

Cover design: Gnibel
Text design and typesetting: Casey Hooper Design

To my wife, Maureen,
for her gifts of encouragement and love,
and to our sons, Wesley and Alan,
who said, "Go for it, Dad."

CONTENTS

PREFACE

After my first article for *Home Digest* was published, in 1997, the editor, Bill Roebuck, said I should write a regular column and suggested "Pen Point" as the title. I was really pleased to have the opportunity and loved the title he picked. I love pens, particularly fountain pens. When I write with them, ideas seem to flow as easily as the ink.

I've enjoyed writing the columns over the years since and have been surprised and pleased by the number of people who have taken time to send me notes in response to them.

I've had one difficulty. Whenever someone asked, "What do you write about?" the best answer I could come up with was simply, "I just write articles." Now I've found a better answer. As I updated and revised the columns in preparation for publishing this book, I discovered a connecting theme.

Most of the time when we look at "reality," it is like looking in a mirror. What is reflected back to us is heavily conditioned by what we have experienced, what is on our mind, and what we are looking for. In my writing, I've been looking past the regular view reflected back at us — that distorted image — in an attempt to catch glimpses of what is really important.

What a relief. Finally I have an answer to the question, "What do you write about?" and, as it turns out, I found the title for this book as well: *Glimpses Through the Mirror.*

Jim Campbell
Oakville, Ontario

PART ONE
LIFE CAN BE LIKE THAT

"WHY DID YOU DO THAT?"

A very young girl sat on the kitchen floor playing with a pile of sand. The sand pail lay beside her. Her mother, alerted by the silence, checked to see what was going on. One look and she asked, "Why did you do that?"

The daughter, confused by the question, answered honestly, "I don't know!"

The mother's instant reaction was, "There must be a reason!"

The daughter, quickly catching on to the game, tried another reason: "I wanted to make a castle."

The mother, losing her patience, said, "That's no reason to bring sand into the kitchen."

Oops! That reason didn't work. A bit frightened and confused by her mother's game, the little girl cried and said, "I was lonely. I wanted to be in the house with you."

Those were magical words. The mother's anger faded away. She got her daughter to help clean up "the mess" and to agree there would be no more sand in the kitchen.

The daughter learned two important lessons.

First: You need to have a reason for what you do.

Second: It needs to be an acceptable reason.

This game, deeply rooted in society, is one we all know how to play.

"I just felt like goofing off" is not an acceptable reason for skipping work. "I was burning out. I needed time by myself" is acceptable.

"I just wanted out" isn't an acceptable reason to end a relationship. But "I discovered we were drifting apart, that our relationship was not meaningful" will probably save you from a lot of criticism.

It's the biggest game around. We all play it and act serious about our reasons, yet secretly we know it is just a game. We know most of the time there is no logic in what we do or say. We just do it or say it. So when we're asked why, we often scramble to invent acceptable reasons.

Happily, we know the game and society's handy-dandy list of acceptable reasons to explain almost anything we do. Like:

"I am overworked, stressed out."

"She doesn't understand me."

"I need to experience life."

"It is in my genes; it runs in the family."

"They never gave me a chance."

Well, you know the sort of standard explanations we give for the dumb things we do and say.

There are sophisticated rules to the game. The most important rule: If you want someone to buy your "acceptable reason," you have to buy theirs. It is only fair. Actually, often it's easy to see through the reasons to the selfishness, carelessness, and fear at the root of behaviour. But if we expose someone's motives, we run the risk that they'll expose *our* hidden agendas. We don't want that so we play by the rules and the game goes on.

Experienced players, knowing that what they're going to do or say might be criticized, find it helpful to figure out acceptable reasons beforehand. Like complaining of a sore back before a tennis match, or of a headache before an exam.

So what's wrong with playing the game? Well, we can play it so much we actually take our reasons and excuses seriously. Even though we make them up, we begin to act as if they reflect reality. And soon our bad behaviour, our failures, seem justified and reasonable. And many of society's acceptable reasons can lead us to feel that the cards are stacked against us.

There is a bigger problem with this business of asking why. To ask why supposes that there is a reasonable, understandable answer out there for everything. A French filmmaker spent eleven years interviewing survivors of the Holocaust for a television series he produced. In the programs, he never tried to answer the question of why it happened.

He said, "If one gets involved in asking the question why, if one gets involved in the nexus of possible reasons, one gets sucked into the infinite universe of self-justification."

He's right! How can there be any reasonable, guilt-removing explanation for the Holocaust? And how can there be acceptable excuses for the acts of terrorism and genocide in our time? By asking why, every evil can end up seeming to be reasonable in "the infinite universe of self-justification."

I wish I hadn't asked my boys "Why did you do that?" so often. It would've been wiser to explain why what they did was wrong, harmful, or dangerous than to train them in how to play the game.

Oh well, "Too soon old. Too late smart."

DON'T CONFUSE ME WITH FACTS

I had to see the people having fun at the casino, the ones in the commercials, all smiles and laughter. I drove over for a look-see. I strolled past the people playing the slots, lingered by the poker tables, and stared at the gamblers throwing dice. All the while, I looked for smiles and laughter, for people dancing around the slots and gaming tables. All I found were serious and stressed-out people.

A college in England is setting up a school to train casino operators. They'll have courses for croupiers, dealers, slot machine repairers, that sort of thing. I don't know whether there's a Canadian college that offers similar courses. Tim Dowling, an English columnist, wondered if the professors "mention that the casino is actually an elaborate hoax aimed at persuading people that they are having fun while their money is being pried away from them?" The odds against winning are astronomical. It is all fixed so the casino — or the government — is sure to win in the end.

Don't people know that gambling doesn't produce tons of laughter and that the odds are severely against anyone winning?

Of course they do! They choose to ignore the facts, hoping that maybe, just once, Lady Luck will intervene on *their* behalf.

It's amazing, in this scientific age, how many believe in things that are illogical. For instance, there is no evidence that the movements of the planets affect or determine the course of our lives. And yet, newspapers dare not cease printing horoscopes, and everyone is expected to know their astrological sign. When those who follow the cycles of the planets are asked why, in the face of the evidence, they look to them for guidance, they often give an answer like, "Well, you never can tell ..."

Then there are the fortune tellers and people who claim to have paranormal powers. James Randi, a magician and author, for years posted a $10,000 prize for anyone who could prove they had supernatural powers or insights. The prize was never won.

He said the best tests of the claims people make about their super powers are when magicians, who know how the tricks are done, get together with scientists to work through the claims of psychics and of those who say they can bend spoons by mind power, find lost articles, or foresee the future. These joint efforts inevitably reveal enough solid evidence to expose the fraudulent claims of mysterious powers.

However, many people are not confused by facts. The real question is not about what can be proved or disproved but about what people want to believe.

It is convenient and comforting for us to believe there are forces at work in the world that determine our condition and destiny: cosmic waves, emanations, luck, and fate. If forces set the course of life, what happens is never our fault. If the course of our life is in the hands of fate, luck, and chance and we can't change the future, why fight it? It's not our fault.

There's a name for that sort of belief. It is fatalism, which, in its various forms, is the oldest faith in the world. However, even the most convinced fatalists try to influence the way things work out. For eons and eons, they have sought ways to influence the forces in control of their destiny so good things happen to them. They try to do things on a lucky day, hold a lucky charm as they roll the dice, have a medium say the right words, follow the same routines, or wear the clothes they wore the last time things went well.

All because, maybe … just maybe … the balance will tip in their favour. They agree that of course it's not logical. "But it's worth a try."

How many people figure that mysterious forces determine their lives? It's hard to say. A lot of people, when things get tough, when they face unexpected outcomes and setbacks, when they blunder badly, easily revert to blaming fate, chance, and powers as responsible.

It is not a good place to be. Fatalists seldom learn from their errors; they are handicapped in coping with unexpected outcomes and in meeting the unknowable future.

Sadly, all have times when we don't want to be confused by the facts. When I get that way, I always make dumb choices. I hate it when there is no one to blame but myself.

LIVING WITH A PARADOX

There is a story about a retired Rabbi who was asked to mediate a conflict between two members of the congregation. He met with the antagonists separately and said to each one, after hearing their side of the story, "You are right!"

When both antagonists objected that they couldn't both be right, he replied, "That is also right!"

I understand his difficulty; it is hard to find the truth. But this story is also about paradoxes.

A paradox is a statement that holds two beliefs as valid when it is logically impossible for both to be right. How can opposing opinions be equally correct? Are paradoxes only a debater's trick, or a lot of mumbo-jumbo?

No!

Actually, we manage to live quite easily with paradoxes. For example, take the age-old question about what makes people tick.

One answer is that, one way or another, who we are is determined by internal and/or external forces. Followers of Freud theorize that we are controlled by forces deep in our subconscious.

However, at the same time that Freud was developing his theories, social scientists were concluding that the environment — where we are born and how we are raised — is what drives our life story.

These days, biologists have entered the debate. After probing the nature of the human genome, they have come to the conclusion that our nature is determined by our genes. Our health, weaknesses, strengths, and character (or lack of it) are all coded in our DNA. It seems that every week or so we are informed that another human disease or fragility is caused by yet another mixed-up bit of genetic code. Indeed, some predict the labs will eventually discover bits of code responsible for love and belief in God.

What we have, as a result, is a lot of ammunition for saying, when we mess up, "It is not my fault."

This is not a new or a particularly scientific idea. It may be comforting to have scientific support for the idea, but, in one form or another, long before the scientific age, hordes of people have argued that we are not in control of who we are. (Interestingly, and paradoxically, we don't mind taking credit for the good stuff we do.)

I'll bet when our ancestors gathered around the fireplace, they said things like:

"He never had a chance with a father like that."

"Poor dear, you can't blame her. Something should have been done to keep her out of that crowd."

"There has to be something painful in their experience to make them so wild."

"He was born under a bad star."

So, for generations there has been an understanding that wrongdoers, outcasts, and failures are, in a deep sense, victims, and that they need sympathy.

Now, let's look at the other side of the paradox.

Our society, at great expense, maintains a huge justice system: police forces, prosecutors, defence lawyers, judges, and a complex variety of sentences. This system rests firmly on the proposition that people are in charge of their own lives and, thus, are responsible for what they do. If we offend, we can be arrested, charged, and convicted, then fined or incarcerated. The rule of law is built on the pillar of responsibility.

How can we live with such a paradox? By using common sense!

Most people define common sense as a body of knowledge common to everyone. We continue to think this way in spite of overwhelming evidence that many people have a very strange sense of right and wrong and of what constitutes acceptable behaviour.

The root meaning of "common sense" is from the word "community." It doesn't refer to what *everyone* knows, but what the *community* knows: what the community has learned over years, decades, and eons.

What the community knows about human behaviour is that both sides of the paradox are true. We know this not from philosophy or science but from personal experience and (mostly) personal knowledge. We live the paradox; we live with powerful forces pushing one way or another *and* with the knowledge that we don't have to let ourselves be pushed around. We know we have a hand in our own destiny. We have choices to make; we can set the path.

It is sad when any of us loses the struggle, and we understand. The struggle is never easy. So we offer our sympathy even as we hold people responsible.

It is a paradox. But it is also common sense.

CAN I BE HONEST WITH YOU?

The ruin of the ancient Forum is a must-see for every visitor to Rome. There the guides will tell you about gladiators fighting to the death and how their fate was often decided by a vote from the crowds in the stands. They will recount how the crowds cheered when prisoners, often Christians, were forced into the ring to be killed by hungry lions and tigers. People from all classes came to laugh at the victims and cheer at their death. It was a day out with drinks and refreshments on sale.

We shouldn't allow ourselves to feel superior to the Romans. We have our hockey, boxing, wrestling, and extreme fighting matches that draw large audiences who cheer the winners and jeer the losers. Blood is often spilled in the rink or on the canvas. When someone is seriously injured or dies, it is passed off with the comment, "That's to be expected."

Another echo from the Roman Forum surfaces on TV in reality shows such as *American Idol* and *Canadian Idol*. The studio audiences are pumped up to cheer the winners and jeer at the losers; they are often cruel in responding to a poor performance.

Maybe they take their lead from the judges, who seem to take downright pleasure in a contestant's failure. In a clip on YouTube from one of the *American Idol* shows, a judge tells a contestant her performance was "extraordinary," then, after a pause for effect, as the woman's eyes are sparkling with joy, he says, "extraordinarily bad." The audience explodes in laughter; the woman is devastated. The judge could have been kinder. He probably would justify his action by saying he was only being honest.

Thankfully, not many of us get exposed to such public criticism. Yet I suspect we've all faced some pretty harsh criticism in our time. It usually comes after someone says something like, "I hope you won't be upset, but can I be perfectly honest with you?"

In the past, my response to such a request has been to tell the person to go ahead. I should be able to handle the truth, I tell myself. A mature person should be able to take honest criticism and learn from it.

So I braced myself for what was to come, telling myself to keep calm, listen carefully, and be sure not to react negatively. I didn't always accomplish all those things.

It has taken me a while to figure some of this stuff out and to acquire some level of objectivity. For example, most people who say they want to be perfectly honest really just want to talk about themselves. Their rant is pretty much all about them and little about me. They give a catalogue of their needs, hurts, disappointments, and frustrations and complain about how their experience, education, and skills are undervalued.

It may be helpful to know this sort of thing about someone, but there's probably little anyone can do to transform such person's version of reality. So I've concluded that, on most of these occasions, I was just in the wrong place at the wrong time.

Marcus Aurelius, philosopher and Roman emperor, had a couple of telling phrases on the subject: "... Candour affected is a dagger concealed ... The feigned friendship of the wolf is the most contemptible of all ..."

He said a real friend would never ask for permission to be frank and honest. True friendship is about compatibility, honesty, and sharing one's thoughts and feelings. Therefore, when someone requests to be allowed to be honest, they are, in effect, denying the friendship and admitting that they have not been truthful with you in the past.

The emperor, who had to be alert for enemies, saw a request for permission to be honest as evidence that the person asking could be a rival with a "dagger concealed" in their words of friendship.

So now I'm working on a plan. If anyone offers to be "perfectly honest with me," I'll decline the kind offer. "Sorry. I'm in overload with all the stuff I already know about myself. It's kind of you to offer, but no thanks!"

Unlike the contestants on reality shows who want to be celebrities, I haven't volunteered to be lavishly praised or abused by critics.

THE IMPORTANCE OF TRUST

We have one of those wide-screen TVs. It is only an inch or two thick (although newer models are even thinner). It works well and has a great picture. I have no idea how it translates the impulses received from cables and wires into colourful moving pictures. I suspect not many people completely understand the physics on which these marvellous machines are based.

Having this new TV reminded me of my grandmother. Once, when I arrived home late one afternoon from university, she asked me to fix her radio. I told her I was sorry, but I had no idea how to do that.

"Well, what good is a university education if you can't even fix a radio?" was her response.

Wow, that was a profound question. Studying history, philosophy, and psychology certainly hadn't equipped me to deal with vacuum tubes, solenoids, and electronic circuits.

In the Victorian world my grandmother grew up in, curious, intelligent people — even if they lacked the skills to fix the things they used — had a pretty good grasp of how things were made and how they worked. They'd seen blacksmiths making horseshoes or hinges; there was no mystery involved in using oil, candles, and gas lamps to bring light to a room; it was easy to understand how mail got to the right destinations; the new telegraph used a simple switch — a telegraph key — for breaking the current into dots and dashes; and, while steam engines seemed complex, everyone who had boiled a kettle understood how steam is made and how powerful it was.

Basically, the Victorians had a lot of independent control over their lives: If things went wrong, they could make do.

Years ago, I bought *How Things Work*, a book full of explanations about everything from the Doppler Effect to how steel is made. It was my go-to book for answers to my sons' questions.

The latest technology has left the Victorians, and my book of explanations, far behind. I'm left with a lot of unanswered questions. How, in heaven's name, do they make the tiny metal balls in ballpoint pens? How does a memory stick work? How does the printer fire minute drops of ink onto the paper? And how does a GPS work? How many of us have a firm grasp of the technology that gives us smartphones and iPads?

I should probably give up asking such questions. All I get as answers are: "You plug the memory stick into a USB port," or "Use the remote and go to the main menu on the TV," or "Hit the print button" or " Pay the Geek Squad $250, and they'll get your TV up and running."

We have become dependent on technicians, call centres, electronic networks, and the "cloud" — whatever that is. If the stuff fails, even for a few minutes or hours, we feel betrayed. If there's a power blackout, we are totally helpless.

In our inability to understand the technology and complexities we rely on, we've developed a backup strategy. It is called trust. We trust the people who know to keep the products going and the systems working. We trust that the promises, performances, and prices will be honest, true, and fair.

One thing I learned from studying history is that the people who have information — people in the know — have a lot of power, and those who are not in the know are exceedingly vulnerable. I suspect a lot of people, corporations, and politicians are not all that interested in honouring the trust endowed in them. According to an interview of a hedge fund manager I caught on the car radio, the smart brokers who created the funds and sold them were looking for "dumb money."

Trust. Without it, our society would grind to a halt.

Let's be honest, no one stops to read what the fine print says on the forms they sign before having an operation, getting insurance, or starting an investment plan, nor the ultra-fine print on product guarantees or sales brochures. If we read them all, and got every question answered, the whole system would grind to a halt. Most of us simply sign: an act of trust in the midst of the complexities of our lives.

This puts a different spin on the ancient Latin saying *caveat emptor* (let the buyer beware). Today, more than ever, one's signature is evidence not of knowledge but of an act of trust. We need to shift the burden of responsibility to *caveat actor* (let the doer beware).

IT'S OKAY NOT TO SMILE

If you've ever seen my picture, for example as printed at the end of my magazine columns, you'll have figured out I'm one of those who go rigid when someone suggests smiling for the camera. I'm basically cheerful. I laugh and smile a lot. But turning a photogenic smile on — that is not easy for me.

Happily, it is not genetic. Our teenage granddaughters can turn on lovely smiles for the camera. They can even do the pose: You know, the glance over the shoulder, the sultry look, that sort of thing. Well, they are teenagers. Anyway, I'm right at home with the "no smiling" policy for passport pictures.

Once, in a TV studio, I watched the show's host. When he got the signal to start, he turned on a thousand-watt smile, and, when the light on the camera went off, so did his smile. Smiling is a big deal in our society, not just for TV hosts. Advertisements promote dentists as people who produce smiles and there's not a word about cavities. The hygienist at my dentist's office offered to give me a whitening treatment. I told her it would be a waste on me; I'm not into full-tooth smiles.

Models on the runways affect painfully serious looks. My theory is that they worry that smiling might ignite waves of laughter at the humorous clothes they have to wear. But almost everyone else in the public eye is expected to smile: airline hostesses, clerks in stores, nurses and doctors in hospitals, and, of course, politicians. The word is that every customer, client, or voter must be greeted with a smile.

On a recent trip, the Passenger Relations Officer on our cruise ship was having a very rough day. To be clear, she was having a horrid day. It was the last day of the cruise, the ship was going to dock nine hours behind schedule, everyone's disembarking plans were disrupted — air flights, bus connections, hotel accommodations, everything. Her job was to fix all the problems.

Her solid smile never wavered. It was amazing! She was confronted by long lines of passengers who were concerned, worried, and apprehensive, and by angry ones who seemed to believe the Pacific gale we'd sailed through for three days up the West Coast had been specifically designed to mess up their lives. Her smile was unwavering, even relentless. Like the Duracell bunny, it just kept going and going.

Smiles are great. They add a lovely lightness to our days and they add a measure of comfort when strangers meet. I smile a lot when greeting, meeting, and chatting with people. (I was once told I "work a room" like a politician — ouch!) Apparently in Japan they are training therapists to help people learn how to smile in order to ease the mental stress caused by work and social pressures.

The difficulty in our smiley culture is that *not smiling* is working its way to becoming an anti-social act: a sign of a bad attitude. Sure as night follows day, sit quietly with a calm or serious countenance and people will say things like: "What's the matter? Not feeling well? Why the frown? Come on now, life's not that bad."

Many have observed, with dismay, that smiles are rarely seen on people as they make their way to work in the morning. Is that a puzzle? For heaven's sake, riding crowded transit vehicles, fighting the morning rush hour traffic, wondering what today's challenges and e-mails will do to you in the next eight hours, these are not the ingredients of a smile.

I'm sure many of us would have felt better if the Passenger Relations Manager had got rid of her smile. It would have conveyed the message that she understood and took our concerns seriously about airline connections and contacting the families and friends who had arranged to meet us.

Why not allow our faces to communicate in a natural way? To show when we are happy, concerned, calm, hurt, glad, or sad? It's like truth in advertising. Maybe we should put up a few signs: "It is okay not to smile."

Anyway, I'm ready for the next passport photo.

THE LESSONS OF BABEL

Long ago, before writing, maybe even before songs, and certainly before people used fire, stories were invented: stories to entertain others, to record the past, to teach survival skills to the young, and, in time, to examine and cast light on deep and complex questions like creation, the nature of evil, honour, truth, courage, and even governance.

Before there were books, schools, philosophies, or history, stories preserved and transmitted the collective wisdom of tribes, communities, and nations down through the years. When writing was invented, some of the first things recorded were these stories containing the wisdom of the generations. One of them was the story of the Tower of Babel.

It is a great story about how the people of a city decided to build a huge tower, one higher and grander than anyone had ever imagined, reaching to heaven. The tower would demonstrate for all time how great and powerful they were.

They never got the tower completed. You probably recall that the reason given in the story for this failure is God's jealousy of the builders' power, causing him to create confusion by having everyone speak different languages. A great many set the story of the Tower of Babel aside as a primitive explanation of how the world's languages got started and an example of the arbitrary ways of God in dealing with the human race.

Well, the gist of the story is not about the invention of languages or the ways of God. And the story is not about times past. It is about the fatal errors that societies, nations, and movements make.

In the story, the community of tower makers discovered that, while individuals were weak, collectively they were mighty. They could build city walls, irrigation systems, and towers. They believed in themselves; they believed there was nothing they could not accomplish. In rapt admiration of themselves, they began the biggest, grandest, most magnificent tower the world had ever seen.

The story is about why they failed. In those days, they gave God the credit (or the blame) for the comeuppance. But God's intervention was not needed. The tower builders were infected with arrogant pride, what the Greeks called hubris and saw as a tragic flaw. They admired themselves, worshipped the community, and were sure they were the biggest, wisest, and brightest — a huge cut above the rest of humanity.

When this sort of thing happens, there are predictable results. The community, the government, or the nation can easily slide into immoral behaviour. They allow injustices to persist (for the common good) and often demand that individuals give total obedience to the group, even to the point of sacrificing their lives. Leaders get away with such demands, often going unchallenged a long time, as they claim to be acting on behalf of the community for the common good. This directs the blame and responsibility away from the leaders to each citizen. In turn, the citizens — each one of them carrying only a small percentage of the blame — feel little pressure to do anything.

People can be moral; movements almost never are. With such freedom of action in their hands, movements, parties, empires, nations, religious groups, and cults all bear within themselves the seeds of their own destruction.

In the story, the builders failed because God impeded their ability to communicate by getting them to talk different languages. The storytellers thus tucked a bonus into the story, an explanation of why there are so many languages. The truth is, divine intervention is never needed to create confusion. We're good at that sort of thing ourselves. Breakdowns of communication, even between people who talk the same language, happen all the time, in every home, office, workplace, club, and family.

Understanding is forever being thwarted by conflicting agendas, by pride, or by envy. Toss in an ample supply of differing interpretations of what words and instructions mean; add a measure of rigid loyalty to a party, philosophy, or cause; stir in a good measure of conflicting remembrances of the past — and the recipe is complete. As a result, people easily get at cross-purposes, and agreements are hard to come by.

The story of the Tower of Babel is the story of empires, civilizations, nations, churches, and political parties. It's about the seeds of failure and destruction that are planted when these suffer from hubris. The story is as up to date as tomorrow's newscast.

THE WHITE COATS

Advertisers know their business. When they promote a product like headache remedies, make-up, computers, or dog food, they suit the actors up in white lab coats. Their "scientific" studies have told them that we believe scientists deal with objective truth and are not subject to such obvious human failings as prejudice, emotion, and self-interest.

The advertisers also tap into our faith that someday science will answer all our physical and social problems. To cater to that hope, news reports usually include stories about yet another discovery or breakthrough.

Scientific experiments follow a basic four-step process. First, the scientists define a question they want to answer and think is answerable. Then they devise an experiment they believe will produce the information they need. Next, they do the experiment, measuring and recording the data they think are important. Finally, they sit down to interpret and evaluate the data to determine if the question they started out with has been answered.

Now that's too brief an explanation, but it is enough to bring out an important point: There is nothing impersonal about science. From asking the question to interpreting the data, it is a human exercise. For example, a news report about what the Hubble telescope had discovered generated a letter to the editor. The writer pointed out that telescopes discover nothing; astronomers who use the telescopes are the ones to make discoveries. Without people, the Hubble telescope is just a complex tube floating in space.

Like law, politics, education, and religion, science is an intensely human activity, and it should be subject to all the same scrutiny and healthy skepticism given to any human endeavour. Science doesn't exist in a vacuum. It is a rigorous human activity. There can be faulty theories, bad questions, and results that are notoriously complex and hard to analyse. The process is hardly objective.

A few years ago, editors of many medical journals in Britain called for "… an independent body to counter fraud, plagiarism and other misconduct committed by doctors and scientists in their eagerness for academic status." Wow!

Actually, it shouldn't surprise us. It seems easy, in scientific forums or in court cases that need expert testimony, to line up experts to present proofs for both sides of any question (that smoking is not harmful … that ecological damage from massive oil spills is soon healed).

What is seldom discussed is how the quality of science depends on the quality of the people, the social climate, the questions asked, the source of the funds, and the political climate both inside and outside the scientific community. There needs to be as much discussion about integrity, ethics, character, and morality in science as in any other field of human endeavour.

Like so many others, I'm grateful to all the scientists who have given my doctors excellent equipment and better drugs. I'm happy that my car is safer, that my computer beats a typewriter by a country mile, and that we have so much information about space and about ourselves.

As grateful as we are, though, we need to be skeptical about all the breakthroughs, discoveries, and the latest wonders that are announced. We need to be critical.

Last winter, millions and millions of snowflakes fell on my small property. I know because it seemed I shovelled a billion of them last January. Well, the word is that no two of them are alike in the whole world. It's a conclusion based on the fact that no one has ever found two the same. With hundreds of billions of snowflakes falling every winter all around the world, who can look at them all? So is it a theory, a working assumption, or an educated guess?

Probably a lot of the stuff we're led to believe is questionable. There are likely lots of questions that never will be resolved.

That's okay. The important thing to know is that the men and women in the white lab coats are just like us. They can be right or wrong, honourable or dishonourable, ethical or scurrilous. We shouldn't let the lab coats fool us.

Say, now that I think of it, I haven't seen a doctor dressed in a white lab coat for years. Maybe the scientists in their labs have discarded them, too. Maybe the TV guys are out of date. Oh well, no matter, whatever sells.

ARE WE DOOMED?

At the movie theatre, we sat through the interminable commercials and promos for upcoming features. Afterward, we agreed on three things: The theatre is taking unfair advantage of its captive audience via these commercials; the sound blasted out is far too loud; and, based on the previews of the many upcoming films, present-day moviemakers have a dismal view of the future.

It seems that, for them, the future is dark, filled with tyranny, hardship, and oppression — plagued with mindless violence and endless destruction. The only hope is that a hero or heroine will overcome the enemy — an enemy which is invariably a "system" that has allowed itself to be corrupted. Certainly, amidst the ruins of unbelievable destruction, the movie hero wins the battle. But one is left with the sense that the victory is temporary. Human frailty, the lust for power and wealth, and corrupted institutions will take over again.

There is a word to describe this view of the future: "dystopia." It's the opposite of "utopia" (from Greek roots meaning "no place"). The word "utopia" was coined by Sir Thomas More. It's the title of his book, in which he sets out the qualities of an ideal society, a fictitious "perfect place."

It's remarkable! You see, More was Henry VIII's point man in that king's tumultuous conflict with the Pope. In those days, nothing was neat and tidy. There were no guideposts to mark the way forward, and decisions were made on the fly. Sadly, More ended up being beheaded in 1534, but that's another story. More's vision has never been fulfilled and probably never will be. Nevertheless, the idea he proposed, that things could and should be better — the idea of progress — has endured for generations.

The last five hundred years of Western society could be seen as a long struggle for progress, equality, and justice. It wouldn't be wrong to say that the drive to make things better is a defining characteristic of our society.

The idea of progress is not confined to social, technological, and economic development. Progress was also what individuals and families strived for. People worked, through education and discipline, to be better and to live better lives. Through war and peace, prosperity and depression, through plagues, storms, floods, and all sorts of setbacks and troubles, people looked for, and worked hard to produce, better days and a better future.

Are the dismal, dystopian movies *just* stories? Or could it be that they reflect a growing mindset in our society? Have psychoanalysis and the biological mapping of the human genome convinced us that we can't fight the way we were brought up or what we were born with, giving us terrific excuses for our failures?

The problems facing our world are numerous: global warming; the proliferation of nuclear weapons; the possibility that an "overdue pandemic" will strike; the clash of cultures and civilizations; and the growing world population pressing on the known limits of the Earth's resources. Also, today's news reminds us how power-hungry, greedy, and dishonest people can destroy nations and great corporations. But are these challenges any worse than those faced by other generations?

Many futurists say the Golden Age is over and the future will not be about reaching for utopia but about accommodating ourselves to dystopia. The wise will anticipate this and protect themselves. But are we doomed? Should the hopes and dreams of generations be set aside? Has the ground under our society severely shifted?

One of history's lessons is that nothing is fixed and very little can be known about the future. So whatever the futurists predict will happen may be interesting but is not of great importance. What matters is the way we encounter the unknowable future. Are we a people who will continue to strive to create a utopia? Are we going to make the future or will it make us? What we believe about the future is important.

It is something like that self-fulfilling prophecy business. Self-fulfilling prophecies come to pass because individuals and societies have a dream of the future and, almost without being aware of it, make the decisions and plot the courses that will bring that future into being. The dream and the vision set the course.

So what is our dream, our vision of the future? Dystopia, a dark and brutal future of endless struggle and violent conflict? Or utopia, as we reach for a better society and world? Upon the answer rests the future.

ON A SCALE OF ONE TO TEN

Every few weeks, I receive a phone call to take part in an opinion survey. "It will only take a few minutes, just a few questions …" Experience has taught me they usually take longer than they say, and that the questions are too hard.

"On a scale of one to ten, how do you rate this government program? Our education system?"

"How do you feel about the quality of your telephone service? Are you 'Very unhappy,' 'Somewhat unhappy,' 'Happy,' 'Somewhat happy,' or 'Very happy' with the service?"

What's the difference between "happy" and "very happy"? Is giving a rating of seven significantly different from giving a six or an eight? I usually give "seven" when asked for a one-to-ten answer. Having a favourite number saves a lot of time.

Actually, surveys are all about numbers. They change our "unhappy" into a number because numbers are easier to deal with. You can add, multiply, and divide numbers to "seasonally adjust" them, to turn them into percentages, and, this being the most fun, to compare them with other numbers. Besides, numbers look impressive, scientific, and honest. They give off an aura of authority.

We love our numbers and percentages; we are obsessed with measuring things and collecting statistics. We seldom question them.

At lunch once, during a time when corporate scandals were filling the news pages, someone said, "Those CEOs are only in it for the money!"

"Actually, only 41.6 percent of them," I said quietly.

No one questioned my invented statistic. I don't suppose many statistics are invented out of nothing, but I think we should question more of them.

I'm sure the people who give us all the percentages and statistics can do the math: add, subtract, multiply, and cast percentages. But the numbers are only as good as the questions being asked. Is the question framed to get certain responses? Is the question too big or complex for a "one to ten" judgment? Who is asking the question? Why? What is the answer they are looking for? A healthy dose of skepticism would serve us well as people pop numbers, percentages, and statistics at us day after day.

There is more to it than the possibility of misinformation or the distortion of facts. Numbers are too impersonal. For example, each year-end, the newspeople report on the number of murders in the year past and start a new count for the New Year. Before they leave the old year, they give the percentage up or down for the year. Obviously up is bad, down is good. If I were an editor, I'd publish a list of every one of the victims for the year, with details about the causes, the families, and the community impact. Numbers are just numbers. People are flesh and blood.

Numbers are used to encourage childish attitudes about what is right and wrong or good and bad. The key argument used by teens in permission-seeking bouts with their parents is, "Everyone is going … everyone else is wearing them … everyone else's parents say it is okay." If "everyone is doing it," it must be all right.

Those who have endured such arguments have good comebacks: "Everyone can be wrong. A stampeding herd can race over a cliff. Lemmings can race to the sea and their death." Even the old adage declaring that "fifty million Frenchmen can't be wrong" is not valid. Values, what is right and wrong and good or bad, have nothing to do with the percentage of people for or against them. They stand alone.

With all this common sense on our side, you'd think we'd be immune from the herd instinct. However, advertisers, politicians, opinion makers, and spin doctors know that telling people what "everyone" believes, does, wants, or hopes sells products, gets votes, and changes opinions and outcomes.

Why are people so easily manipulated by the numbers game? For the same reason teenagers watch what everyone is doing. They want to belong, to fit in, to be "with it" and up to date.

I try to remember that, while being part of a group is good, letting any group of people determine our values isn't. It is not good to hand over our moral principles to anyone else. Oh, and I'm not doing any more surveys. On a scale of one to ten, I give them a zero.

THE TALKING WOUNDED

When I was eight, I marched into the kitchen to tell my mother, "Dad has no thumb on his right hand!"

She gave me a look that expressed amazement and patience. My dad's right hand and wrist were mangled in a printing press well before they got married. The doctors did their best to patch things up. He ended up with very limited flexibility in that hand and no thumb.

It wasn't that I was unaware of all that. It was just the first time I'd ever thought about what it meant not to have a thumb and a working right hand. For days I watched how my father did simple tasks and then experimented doing things without using my right thumb. I tried to write with a pencil between my index and middle fingers and to hold a knife and fork that way to cut meat. Everything I tried was hard, really hard.

I now understand why I'd never really thought about his handicap. He never talked about his injury or complained about the way it had changed his life and prospects. He managed; he compensated; he carried on.

In Rosemary Sutcliff's novel *The Eagle of the Ninth*, a Roman centurion — who had suffered a career-ending leg wound — said to a man he had freed from slavery: "Are you going to live all the rest of your life as though you had taken a whipping and could not forget it? Because if you are, I am sorry for you. You don't like being a freed-man, do you? Well I don't like being lame. That makes two of us, and the only thing we can do about it, you and I, is to learn to carry our scars lightly."

Many people overflow with bitterness at the hand they have been dealt in life and continually recount the details of their misfortune, of their handicap. The cursed thing that happened curses them every day. They are the "talking wounded."

Long ago, Emperor Marcus Aurelius said that remembering our grievances and adding them to our personal grief list hurts our ability to deal with difficulties as they occur. Adding up injuries puts a heavy load on every small injury and difficulty. As a Stoic, Marcus Aurelius believed nothing we encounter should touch our spirit. We should act as if nothing had happened and treat the good, the bad, and the in-between with equal distain.

I don't think that would work very well. If you have a withered leg from polio, a gimpy hand, asthma, acute anxiety, whatever, there is no sense denying that reality. Denial won't help you deal honestly with life or your abilities.

How we deal with handicaps is important. Because, when I last checked, no one is perfect. Everyone has flaws and handicaps of one sort or another. While some never tire of telling the story of how their limitations have kept them from living a full life and how unfair it all is, others stoically simply soldier on.

Stephen Hawking, the brilliant physicist who has suffered from ALS (Amyotrophic Lateral Sclerosis, or Lou Gehrig's disease) for decades, has said: "One has to be grown up enough to realize that life is not fair. You just have to do the best you can in the situation you are in."

The "best you can" for Sam Sullivan, confined to a wheelchair, was to become Vancouver's mayor; for Stephen Fletcher, as a quadriplegic, it was to be parliamentary secretary to the Minister of Health.

People like these point the way for all of us to deal with handicaps.

Ah, you say, but they are exceptional people. Not really. They did what many have done. They made two solid choices.

First, they were absolutely honest with themselves and with their reality. They saw that dwelling on their loss was counterproductive. Their handicaps would not go away. The wheelchair, the limp, or the weakness was part of their future.

Second, they decided to move on, to concentrate their thoughts and energy on what they could do rather than on what they couldn't.

It is hard to do that, but I suspect that most people with handicaps find that they must accept their reality and move on. It is not easy to have a crushed hand, to carry your scars lightly, but there is a life to live.

BUTTONS AND BOWS AND BRACELETS

At a conference a while ago, everyone seemed to be wearing buttons with messages supporting all kinds of worthy projects and causes. Some of the delegates were festooned with so many buttons it was obvious they had left no good cause unturned. I was prepared. I made myself a big button. It was blank: It bore no printing, no message, no graphics.

To the inevitable question, I replied, "I want to be involved, but I can't make up my mind."

I received a variety of responses and comments. A few people laughed, many wondered at my weird sense of humour, and a few seemed genuinely concerned about the level of my compassion.

To my surprise, one of the conference leaders insisted I give him the button. To this day, I wonder how he incorporated it into his presentations. Did he use it for a bit of comic relief or as a serious illustration of how some people opt out of helping solve society's problems? Probably it was the latter; he was an uptight kind of guy.

I don't get to go to many conferences these days, but I imagine delegates still wear buttons to show their concerns, compassion, and support. But maybe not. The buttons may have been replaced by ribbons looped like little bows and pinned to coats, jackets, blouses, and sweaters.

Ribbons of all colours: red, green, yellow, white, and blue. And for every cause, illness, and charity. Wearing one of them is a public statement of one's commitments and passions. The same goes for those Lance Armstrong–type bracelets. Distinctive at first, there seems to be one for almost every cause.

There has been another change. While the buttons handed out at conferences were mostly worn while the meetings and conferences were in session, these, along with ribbons and bracelets, are now part of many people's daily attire. Some wear them all the time, even onto the podium at the Academy Awards.

People use them to bear steadfast witness to their empathy for the suffering of others. With so many ribbons and bracelets and so many causes and concerns, it's difficult to remember what the colours represent. Is red about drunk driving, green for the environment, and white to protest violence against women? I'm sure I don't have the causes and the colours right.

The ribbons and bracelets are a sign that our inventive society is in the process of creating new ways of expressing empathy and compassion and of showing new styles for collective responses to social problems, grief, and loss. It is now common, since the death of Princess Diana, for memorials of cards, stuffed animals, and bouquets of flowers to spring up at the scene of a tragedy or to mark the passing of a celebrity.

Bruce West, a researcher for the British think tank Civitas, which studies our society's customs and the direction our society seems to be moving, calls these new ways "conspicuous compassion."

The popularity of wearing ribbons and creating instant memorials seems to be clear evidence that we are caring people. However, West's analysis of the data indicates that these public displays of empathy for the poor, the homeless, the dispossessed, and the bereaved have not engendered very much compassionate action.

He must have something there. In our communities, all kinds of volunteer organizations, service clubs, churches, charities, and social agencies suffer from declining pools of volunteers.

Sure, there may be all sorts of reasons for this decline. People are working longer hours, husbands and wives are both working, the pressures of the twenty-first-century business world are mounting. It's sad to need excuses while blood banks plead for donors, transplant lists grow ever longer, teams need coaches, kids need Big Brothers and Big Sisters, and hospitals and major charities have to turn to lotteries to raise money. (By the way, lotteries don't have much to do with compassion or empathy. The major concerns of ticket buyers are the odds of winning and the prizes offered, not heart and stroke victims, cancer research, or hospital funding problems.)

Compassion, like all the important virtues — love, faithfulness, patience, honour, truth, and justice — exists only within actions. Compassion is not about signs and symbols but about the nature of our deeds. Without action, deeds, and generosity, compassion has no substance, no existence.

I guess all we need is a reality check. Great things can happen if we all make sure to stand behind our words and live up to all our buttons and bows and bracelets.

WHY ARE THERE SO MANY COMPLAINERS?

I've been reading the newspaper, listening to talk shows on radio and TV, and hearing what politicians and commentators are saying about the way things are in this country.

Here is the message I'm getting: "The government in Ottawa doesn't know what it is doing; the waiting times in Emergency at the hospital are horrendous; getting an appointment with a specialist is a struggle; we live under the threat of disintegration as every region follows Quebec's lead and threatens to play the separation card; traffic is a disaster; some grads from high school have poor basic literacy skills; the courts are slow, prisons are packed, and the parole system is a disaster." We seem surrounded by an atmosphere of discontent.

It all makes you wonder how Canada consistently ranks as one of the best-run countries on the planet. Why do thousands risk everything to come here to live? Why are there so many complainers?

Well, some people are serial complainers. Their insights into wrongs and nascent disasters fill their every conversation. They have nothing good to say and plenty bad to say: "They should have known better … have foreseen the problem … They are idiots." Spending a few minutes with people like this can make the best of days depressing.

And yet, they are simply an extreme element in a basic atmosphere of criticism that's built into our society. We are expected to have opinions, to be critics about almost everything: dinner menus and service; the first act of a play; the latest style; the colour of a room.

We're also expected to have intelligent positions on nuclear power, on which movie deserves an Oscar, on which political party is the best. We're expected to have lucid explanations to justify our opinions and choices. So, in our culture, we are programmed to be critical.

This emphasis on criticism distorts our view of reality and our ability to enjoy our lives. Our fault-finding habits dull our sense of gratitude and appreciation.

We've come a long way, a very long way, from the days of the Great Depression of the 1930s. Back then there was no employment insurance or universal health care; pensions for the elderly were meager and required a means test; people with jobs worked long hours, plus a half-day on Saturdays, and dared not complain as they struggled to put food on the table.

A dose of this kind of reality is helpful.

However, it is obvious that behind the spate of fault-finding rests a misunderstanding of the way the world works. Society is so connected and interdependent that every change creates new conditions, a new balance. It is something like one of Murphy's

Laws: "Every change produces unintentional, unforeseeable, and unwanted consequences."

What seemed so good and just at the time, or seemed to be a step forward to correct an injustice, often creates more problems. A benefit for one person or social group can bring stress or hardship to others.

Unintentional and unforeseeable consequences are always playing themselves out in real life. It works something like this: Investing in medical science prolongs life for people (good); people live longer (good); this requires the investment of more money in pensions and elder care (bad); this limits a government's ability to fund universities and fill potholes (bad); young people are shortchanged (bad — in fact, a new injustice needing attention).

Of one thing, I am certain: The people responsible for the medical advances never thought about their impact on potholes.

Critics are often deemed to be a pain in the neck. "Criticism is easy, achievement is difficult," said Winston Churchill. "Critics have an obligation to be fair and to offer constructive criticism," said Madeleine Albright. These sentiments are helpful to those who have suffered from the sharp thrusts of mean-spirited critics but don't get at the core problem.

Critics believe they are smart and realistic, but they are mistaken about the nature of the world and the path of progress. Is it smart to ignore the "law of unintended consequences"? Is it realistic to badmouth those who try to make things better, who try to do what is right and just?

How much better it would be to celebrate advances, to recognize every small step forward for what it is: another step on a long journey of fits and starts.

With this figured out, I'm ready for the next character who says our country is going to hell in a handbasket.

WHAT IS CHARITY REALLY ABOUT?

In the popular musical *My Fair Lady*, Professor Henry Higgins transforms Eliza Doolittle, a poor flower girl, into a lady, by teaching her to speak impeccable English. One memorable scene takes place when Eliza's father, Alfred P. Doolittle, turns up at Professor Higgins' house to gain some sort of benefit for being Eliza's father. In a lively discussion, Alfred reveals himself to be a first-class rascal.

"What am I?" he says. "I'm one o' the undeserving poor, that's what I am. Think of what that means to a man … If there's anything goin' an' I ask for a bit of it, it is always the same story: 'You're undeserving, so you can't have it.' "

In Victorian times, the era in which *My Fair Lady* is set, as well as in our time, we're concerned about who is worthy of charity and who falls into the classification of the undeserving. No one wants to be taken advantage of, and charitable donations should not be wasted, so lines are drawn about who is in and who is out.

However, there are important questions about the other side of charity. No, I'm not writing about the possibility of fraud or mismanagement but of concerns about the way the money is gathered to support charities.

The word "charity" began its career in the English language referring to love, a special love driven by selfless compassion, empathy, and a sense of our common humanity. It was an expression of our need for one another, an acceptance of the truth in the old saying, "There, but for the grace of God, go I."

That meaning has evolved over the years to refer to more specific acts of kindness that may, or may not, be so much an expression of compassion as of a sense of duty, what one has to do — one has to do something. And so, while charity has a place on people's to-do lists, it is often devoid of any real commitment.

Charity is what you do when you have a little bit extra, whether it is loose change or bits of time, that won't in any way affect the smooth running of your days. This attitude is so prevalent that, no matter how great the need or how worthy the cause, many charities work hard to convince people that donating even the smallest amount — the loose change — matters.

Well, of course, it all adds up, but the whole process seems to be a long distance from any sense of real compassion and commitment that should be inherent in acts of charity. Don't misunderstand. Tossing a dollar into a battered paper cup held out by someone surviving on the street, or into a Christmas kettle at the mall, are good things. However, they are not a big deal.

It seems many of the big charities have concluded that it is best to downplay compassion and commitment in their appeals for funds. The big health charities have decided to rely on greed and materialism to rake in the big bucks. The magic word is lotteries. The familiar pitch dangles great prizes before our eyes: a dream house, a luxury car, a fabulous cruise, or a million dollars. "Chances of winning are one in three," they proclaim, urging people to "buy now."

Minimal attempts are made in the promotional materials to inform people about health or healing, about compassion and empathy for those suffering, or about commitment to the community. In the lottery promotions, don't expect information on how much is left for the cause from a hundred-dollar ticket after all costs are covered.

Lost in the loose change and lottery business is an important point about charity. It is not only about money. One of the highest expressions of our humanity, charity is also about how we care for one another. Charity is about building relationships and making sure our society is a place where compassion thrives. This is important in a time when people who believe it is a dog-eat-dog world seem to be gaining ground as they drive themselves to rise up in the world.

Thankfully, many people understand the need for charity and put their time, talent, and money to good use. Let us hope that many more of us, who now toss in a bit of loose change or buy the odd lottery ticket, will be inspired to do more and join in to make our world a little bit better.

DAMN NUMBERS

My afternoon walk often takes me past the local elementary school. All the way, the intersections on the route are monitored by crossing guards. The other day, as usual, ten to fifteen minutes before classes were due to be out, mothers from all around the neighbourhood hurried down to the school to pick up their children and escort them safely home.

They do this because they know the streets are dangerous. Every day, children are abducted. The statistics tell the tale: 56,000 children were abducted in Canada in 2004. This reality is reinforced by photos of missing children appearing on billboards and milk cartons.

However, here is a number that is not sensationally reported: of the 56,000 reported abducted, only three were taken by strangers. Three!

For heaven's sake, we don't have a problem with unsafe streets, we have a problem with broken marriages, child custody battles, and separation and divorce settlements that people feel are unjust and inequitable.

Here's another example of trouble with numbers. There was a huge lineup at the lottery kiosk in the plaza. The 649 Lottery's top prize that week was advertised as "one of the biggest jackpots ever." That night, the TV news interviewed some people buying tickets. "What would you do if you won?" they were asked.

They'd pay off debts, travel, invest, give to family members, or (as in the recent TV commercial promoting the lottery) buy cottages on Lake Joseph for all the children.

Ah, how nice it is to dream. One little fact is not featured at the kiosks or in the advertising, however. The odds against winning the lottery, of walking away with the whole package, are astronomical. They are not a million to one, or even ten million to one. The odds for the big payout come in at around fourteen billion to one. That is fourteen followed by nine zeros. The girl next door has a far better chance of marrying a Royal Prince than winning the lottery.

During the Christmas and New Year's holidays, articles surfaced in the papers about how painfully hard the season can be on lonely people, those who remember happier times. The articles were based on reports that the strains of the season are so stressful, there is a substantial rise in suicides. Thus many church congregations hold "Blue Christmas" services, and many clubs and social agencies make a special effort to try to counter this terrible "reality."

Suicide is a major problem. However, in reality, Christmas does not affect the numbers. In December 2003, Dr. Herbert Hendin of the American Society of Suicide Prevention reported, "Suicide does not peak during the winter holidays ... Suicide is linked to mental illness, substance abuse, alcoholism. It is not simply something that is precipitated by some event like losing a girlfriend, or a job that didn't work out."

So how is it so many people believe the opposite?

The generous Canadian response to the tsunami tragedy confirmed our view that we are a generous people reaching out to others. We hear about a million dollars donated to a project, about Canada forgiving a poor country's debt, and our Prime Ministers, when on the international stage, are quick to pledge that we'll work to solve the urgent needs in areas like Africa.

However, there are other numbers. The UN has set a benchmark commitment by prosperous countries like Canada at 0.7 percent of Gross Domestic Product (that's seventy cents for every hundred dollars of GDP).

What do we give? Only 0.28 percent of GDP (that is twenty-eight cents for every hundred dollars of GDP). Oh, yes ... seventy percent of that money comes back to us through jobs and the purchase of goods and services in Canada. So now, let's see ... deduct seventy percent ... that works out that we gave about eight and a half cents, a long way from seventy cents.

I'm not very good at numbers. Maybe that's why I am skeptical when numbers are thrown at us. What I do know is that what a lot of us believe just isn't so.

How come we don't know that only three children were abducted by strangers? Why aren't the lottery odds advertised, and what's with this Christmas suicide myth? Why doesn't the government talk about the stingy eight and a half cents?

Who doesn't want us to know these things? Who profits? Why do I always end up with more questions?

WE HAVE MET THE ENEMY

One of the benefits of getting older is that a lot of history ends up happening in your lifetime. I remember the 1930s, when homeless men camped in "the bush" near our house in Ottawa; the patriotism and determination of people in the Second World War; the first jets, not to mention zippers, Velcro, television, computers, scotch tape, and penicillin — the regular stuff of our lives today. Yes, and there was "the Bomb," the assassination of President Kennedy, the moon landing, and the end of the Berlin wall. Lots of changes.

It has been a fascinating time to be alive and to realize that the unexpected lies in wait at every turn of the road of life. What will be next? Who knows? Changes and innovations follow each other with such rapidity that many declare the only constant these days is change itself.

They are wrong. There is one thing that has not changed in history for generations: the struggle between those who have privilege, wealth, and power and those who don't.

The Magna Carta and the great revolutions, like the French

and Russian ones, arose out of the struggle to have the power and wealth of societies shared. History records the confrontations between the barons and the kings, the merchants and the aristocracy, the landless and the landlords, and the workers and the factory owners. The struggle never ends, because the minute the "have-nots" become the "haves" and enjoy power, wealth, and prestige, they immediately close ranks to protect their newly won position.

The very people who fought for justice, who sang songs about equality, fraternity, and solidarity, find it expedient to stand against anyone who wants them to share. They use their newfound status to pass laws, set standards, and promote customs designed to make their victory permanent. They undertake defensive positions, not only against the class or faction they displaced or forced to make room for them at the top, but also against those who, as they did, are struggling from below to secure a place in the sun.

You can find evidence of these strategies in every age and nation protecting the craft guilds and unions, the aristocracy, the merchants, and the honoured professions. So here is something that never changes: The "haves" prefer the status quo; they like to hold on to what they have acquired.

It is the permanent undercurrent of life: the struggle behind the items that fill our newspapers and political agendas and the issues behind government budgets, tax laws, and subsidies. While the poor nations demand a share in the world's prosperity and justly complain that the rules set by the wealthy are unfair, the gap between the wealthy industrialized countries and the nations of the third world grows bigger.

The division in every nation between the powerful politicians, the corporate elite, and the top ten percent in society versus those who barely get by widens year by year. And so the struggle between the haves and the have-nots — the quest for equality and justice — is a constant in history, a permanent fact of life. It is always there; only the players change from time to time.

Thus the struggle for human rights, justice, and equality is a permanent one. The victories won by our ancestors and our fathers and mothers over oppression and inequality were not won once and for all. They were only brief skirmishes in a never-ending conflict.

Liberty, justice, democracy, and the sharing of wealth are always under attack; there are forces working to wear them away. It is because power, wealth, prestige, and fame produce bitter fruit — no one ever has enough.

What can we do? I suppose the answer depends on which side of the struggle one finds oneself. But what if we find ourselves on *both* sides of the struggle?

We see the need for the people above us, who have so much power to make change, to open up and share. But we feel we need to protect our place in the scheme of things, the position we have earned, and the rewards that have come to us. Which probably means that Pogo, the cartoon figure of a generation ago, was right when he said, "We have met the enemy and he is us."

ARE THEY LISTENING TO US?

The Devil made me do it! At a sort of classy event, I shuffled along the receiving line with all the rest of the people. When I got to the top of the line, as I shared handshakes and the odd hug with the VIPs, I said to each one of them, even the guest of honour, "The elephants are stampeding!"

Each one smiled and said things like, "Isn't it wonderful"; "Yes, it is a fine turnout"; and "Good to see you out tonight." By the end of the line, I needed extraordinary discipline to hold back my laughter. I couldn't believe no one heard what I said.

I feel better having confessed. I promise not to do it again.

Actually, it was a test — a very unscientific one, of course — that proved two things. The first is a comforting bit of information. Don't worry about what to say when you are working your way along a receiving line. It doesn't matter.

The second lesson is also clear: Most of us are not all that good when it comes to listening. It seems there is a huge difference between listening and hearing.

It's easy to understand why the VIPs didn't catch that

"elephants are stampeding" business. If you've ever been on the stationary side of a receiving line, you'll know how it is. It's not just that listening is difficult but that there's simply too much happening, and your first priority is to try to remember names and connections. Receiving lines simply aren't the right setting for receiving information. It's a time for greeting, shaking hands, and hugging.

While all that is true enough, let's be honest. Most of us, in situations less hectic and confused, have been accused of not listening. More people than we can count — husband, wife, teenagers, partners, fellow workers, presidents, and potentates — complain that no one listens to them.

Communicating is actually difficult and frustrating because, for information to be transferred, there needs to be a listener as well as a communicator.

At a meeting a few months ago, I saw the pros at work. The new program was explained in great detail with computer graphics and voice-over slides. Two well-trained speakers repeated the program's start-up date over and over again. I was impressed by their fancy equipment and skill. I had my regular daily struggle with the tenth commandment — you know the one: "Thou shalt not covet." And then I saw the other side. Brief seconds after the presentation ended, the man sitting next to me leaned over and asked, "Did you get the date when all this is supposed to start?"

Listening is hard, and good listeners are very special people.

My wife and I have a friend who is a wonderful listener. It was when she moved away that we really appreciated how important her listening ability had become to us. We would call her when we'd had a bad day, when things were not going well, when we just generally felt rotten, and a few minutes of conversation calmed the waters, improved our judgment, and made us feel better. She wasn't strong on advice or solutions. She never interrupted our story except to interject a few comments like:

"Oh, no!"

"Isn't that terrible!"

"You must be exhausted!"

"She didn't!"

It worked wonders. You felt better. No, it was more than that. You *were* better: better able to cope, to get on with things.

I'm sure one of the most helpful and healing aspects of a visit to a psychotherapist or a counsellor is that they are excellent listeners: They respond to what is said; they encourage one to go on, to say more; and they even take notes.

There are all sorts of courses offered on how to speak in public but very few on how to listen. That's too bad. I'm confident that, most of the time, all we need is to have someone listen to our problems, pains, and perplexities. We don't want advice, solutions, suggestions, explanations, critical analysis, or philosophical opinions. Mostly what we need is just to get it all out, to be heard and understood. When that happens, we feel better and healing begins.

I've talked myself into it. I'm going to try to be a better listener and use more phrases like: "They didn't!" "Oh, no!" and "Well, that's a surprise!" and ease off on advice and opinions. And from now on, I'll behave myself in receiving lines.

REFLECTIONS FROM THE QUIET CORNER

I'm reticent. It is a trait that runs deep with the men in our family. We don't talk very much about our feelings and fears, our griefs and gripes. When I was a little guy and got into crying, my father would say, "That's enough crying now." I soon learned that, while crying was *okay*, it wasn't good to let it go on too long. Mother, when something got lost, broke, or bent, often repeated the old adage, "There's no use in crying over spilt milk."

Maybe it has something to do with our distant family roots in Scotland. Highlanders are reputed to be uncomplaining, use few words, and have long silences. I doubt it was just to save their breath for playing bagpipes (which, of course, would have been a most worthy exercise). No, I think the idea was that too much talking about problems doesn't help much and probably makes things worse.

Those who aren't inclined to talk a lot about feelings have been, in the past twenty years or so, under constant pressure to change. They have been accused of being uptight, putting on false fronts, living in states of denial, and repressing their feelings. That is heavy stuff.

The mainstream idea is that it's dangerous to bottle things up; it's healthy to let out your feelings, rage, and frustrations, and to register every complaint. In the 1960s, they said, "Let it all hang out." The assumption is that if you don't, you'll explode.

Apparently the popularity of the idea that everyone should be open to reviewing pains and problems is rooted in psychiatry with its famous couches. Learning to listen is an important skill to have. Talking things out is helpful for a lot of people. But maybe a little bit goes a long way.

Those who assume everyone needs to talk things out miss an important point. The non-talkers, the quiet ones, are not necessarily in a state of denial. They're certainly not into repressing reality. Their pain, their grief, and their disappointments are real. But they know that all the talking in the world will not change the reality, wipe the slate clean, or recover what they have lost. In fact, they are sure that retelling the stories, describing details of the pain, and explaining the anger would keep the wounds open.

Darius, the ancient King of Persia, knew how to keep anger alive. When he heard that some people called Athenians had burned Sardis, an insignificant city far from Babylon, he ordered his personal servant to repeat, three times before serving every meal, "Master, remember the Athenians." At every meal his anger expanded, and the wound was kept open.

There are lots of people like Darius who choose to keep their wounds open.

There are others who choose a different way. They accept what has happened to them as a fact of their lives, square their shoulders, and move on. They don't expect closure. They don't expect the slate to be wiped clean. They don't expect to forget the past. They refuse to allow the hurt to have a life of its own, to define who they are, to set the daily agenda of their life, or determine the future.

It is comforting, as the as the years add up, to find new studies reporting that reticent people have known something about how to work things out and how to cope with upsets. The latest word from researchers is that controlling your reactions and holding back your emotions or your anger is healthier than expressing them.

Some psychologists say that revisiting your bad feelings can work like an infection, poisoning your spirit. By reactivating hurt feelings, you define yourself as a person who feels awful. And so, when you feel good, you naturally assume it is not the real you.

Letting anger flow probably never clears the air. It actually reinforces and increases the anger. As far as one can tell, people who often vent their anger don't appear to be all that happy or content. They are unhappy because every day, maybe even every meal — as in the case of Darius — is seasoned with anger.

So, how am I doing? Fine! As long as I avoid groups that want me to "talk it out" or "get it off my chest."

"WHATEVER IT TAKES"?

It's that time of year again. The baseball season is in full swing; the professional football teams are getting ready to hit the gridirons … and the Stanley Cup hockey playoffs are still quite fresh in our memories.

It is the time of year when sports writers and broadcasters gather predictable quotes from star players. You know, the regular stuff about how they will have to dig down, play as a team, and be up for the key game. They will also record promises from coaches and managers who declare they'll do "whatever it takes to win."

They are completely serious. They are ready to do anything and cut any corner to build a winning team, get into the playoffs, and be the champs. Look at the salaries the star players are paid and at the attempts to batter good quarterbacks out of the game. And we all know how hockey coaches send tough guys onto the ice to intimidate the opposition, pound other players into the boards, and provoke penalties. Sure, it often results in knocked-out teeth, stitches, and career-threatening concussions and neck injuries. But that's okay; it's considered part of the game. You see the same attitude in the way major league baseball overlooked the use of performance-enhancing drugs in the Home Run Derby a couple of seasons ago.

Sports are an important part of our culture. The attitudes and values they display have a powerful influence. Fair play, dedication, discipline, courage, and steadfastness are extremely important to learn and uphold. But these days, "fair play" seems to have been displaced by "we'll do whatever it takes."

All sorts of people promise to "do whatever it takes" to be a star, to be famous, to get to the top, to make their company successful, or to win an election. It is the prescribed road to success. When a political leadership candidate withdraws from a race because he doesn't want to play such games, or when someone passes up a big opportunity because they feel the cost is too high, the cynics declare them foolish and naïve.

"They could have had it all!" they say. "Isn't that what everyone wants? Isn't that the real bottom line? Don't they know how the world works?"

Philosophers for generations have debated whether the end justifies the means. It is an old debate and isn't likely to be settled any time soon. The benefits in doing "whatever it takes" to reach a high goal seem blindingly obvious. You win the game, improve the bottom line, and maybe become one of the rich and famous. A few compromises and concessions on the way to the goal won't matter once you get to the top.

So what's the problem?

Things can get out of hand. The daily news brings us all sorts of reports of terrorists, dictators, robber barons, or cult leaders who are sure their lofty goals justify sacrifice, disruption, famine, wars, revolution, unemployment, political prisoners, and judicial executions.

But we don't have to cast such a wide net. The problems are closer to home.

It is easy to forget that honesty, truth, justice, fairness, compassion, and love are not deeds. They are qualities given to actions. Qualities can't be stored for later use. If values are not used, they don't exist. And they are not retroactive. If you miss an opportunity to be honest and fair, you can't fix it later. A vicious, career-ending football tackle or hockey check cannot be corrected with compassion and caution later.

The present is all we have. Later never comes. If we are honest, most of know we will never reach the elusive top of the heap. So if that's what we are waiting for before we do the right thing … Well, you see the problem. It may never happen.

Besides, clawing your way to the top develops strong habits. It becomes natural to deal with problems, enemies, and frustration in cold, calculating, selfish ways. It's who you are and it's hard for a leopard to change its spots.

A lot of us seem to have quietly accepted the "whatever it takes to win" philosophy. Maybe we should take time to weigh the benefits and burdens carefully before we go much further. What do you think?

SECOND CHRISTMAS

It is still only fall as I write this, but everywhere plans are being made for Christmas. It is time to start making a list of things to do, because it can be a busy time of the year.

Celebrating Christmas is complicated, because there are actually two Christmas celebrations.

What we could call the First Christmas, the time when Christians mark the birth of Jesus, is an important opportunity to remember the founder of the faith who, like all people, was born of a woman, who was born in humble circumstances into a world of danger and division. Over the years, Christians have created rich traditions and customs and a wealth of glorious music for this celebration.

The Second Christmas is almost completely detached from any religious roots. It is the Christmas of Santa Claus and Christmas trees, of gifts, shopping, parties, Rudolph the Red-Nosed Reindeer, and Jimmy Stewart in *It's a Wonderful Life.*

This secular celebration generates the yearly spending spree many businesses rely on for survival. This Christmas is so popular it is celebrated not only in countries with old Christian roots but in many non-Christian ones such as Japan.

It is not hard to understand why Christians celebrate the birth of Jesus. It is not so easy to figure out why the Second Christmas endures year after year. Heaven knows its excesses and its blatant commercialism are easy targets for every budding social critic.

In their zeal, the critics seldom ask what causes the Second Christmas to endure and grow. To some, the answer is simple. It is promoted and stage-managed by a consortium of advertisers, merchants, and entertainers. Thus the driving force is money. This is the sort of notion promoted by those who believe ordinary people are easily manipulated. Abraham Lincoln had an opinion about that, saying, "... you may fool all of the people some of the time, you can even fool some of the people all the time, but you can't fool all of the people all of the time."

However, I believe there has to be something positive and beneficial in this Second Christmas for it to endure and prosper year after year.

What is special about it? Well, look at what people do at Christmas. They take the opportunity to show they care for one another. They find ways to express their gratitude to those who have helped them through the year. They use the time to connect with friends and relatives through calls, cards, letters, and Christmas parties. Christmas is a holiday when people go out of their way to be patient, kind, and pleasant. When they open wallets and purses to give to those in need.

So the Second Christmas has deep roots in our need to

recognize our interdependence, our debts to others, and our common humanity. To put it another way, people all over the world keep Christmas because it gives them permission to smooth their hard edges and be human, to express honest feelings that are held in check most of the time.

Most of the year there are precious few socially acceptable ways to express positive feelings to those outside our most intimate circle. Give your employee or a friend a gift in July and they'll probably be embarrassed. They may even wonder at your motives, what you want from them, or whether you're feeling guilty.

So Christmas allows us to be human, to express how we feel. It gives us permission to be nice, kind, generous, and appreciative. That is why it is such a wonderful time of the year. We enjoy being kind and pleasant. We enjoy playing our part in the thousands and thousands of kind acts done by all sorts of ordinary people like us. That's why the Second Christmas endures year after year and spreads around the world. It enriches our lives and fulfills basic human needs.

It creates a wealth of good feelings.

And so, accidentally almost, Second Christmas reflects many of the aspects of the Christian Christmas, with its emphasis on love, respect, and compassion and the qualities Christians are to have in their lives.

Sadly, soon after Christmas, the effort to be kind and understanding fades. That's when people say that life is getting back to normal, which is a pretty sad commentary about what life is like the rest of the year and about what we think of as normal.

WORDS ARE POWERFUL

"Sticks and stones may break my bones, but names will never hurt me." In primary school we all learned to use that taunt when someone called us a "name." It was a way to deflect the verbal attack and give the impression you could not be hurt by name-calling. Of course it wasn't true. The names, insults, and cruel comments did hurt. You remembered the words long after the cuts and bruises had healed. Words can cut deep.

Words also have the power to change the way people see and think about things. You see, a lot depends on the words people use. Select the right word, and you can influence the way people understand reality and how they think about life. By the use of words alone, people can make what is bad appear to be good.

You may have heard of the court case in Toronto concerning a department store employee who stalked a woman he worked with. The store was accused of neglecting to take appropriate action on her complaint. Their defence lawyer argued that the man was not a "stalker" but a "persistent pursuer"! To be followed by a "stalker" paints a frightening picture, whereas it is almost romantic to talk of a "persistent pursuer."

A man in the town of Oakville recently wrote to the editor of the local paper complaining that the town council wanted to designate his house as a Heritage Home. If his house becomes a Heritage Home, he will cease to have full control over his own property. He would have to get permission to make any changes.

What you call something makes a big difference. The "swamp" on my property belongs to me. Call it a "wetland" and all of a sudden people begin to see it as a "community resource" and it becomes a concern for environmentalists. Your "lot" at the cottage, where the birds make their nests and the chipmunks scurry around, is yours until someone decides it is a "habitat" and it, too, belongs to everyone. By the way, that tree on your front lawn may not be yours. It is probably classified by your municipality as part of "the urban forest."

Use words carefully, and you can make wrong seem right, or at least acceptable.

The middle-aged parent who leaves family and spouse is not "deserting" their family and responsibilities; they are having a "mid-life crisis." Sounds sort of acceptable.

People who practice really weird, abnormal, and sometimes destructive behaviour — things our ancestors called sins — gloss over what they do by calling it "self-expression" or a "lifestyle."

It seems everything from adultery to prostitution and body piercing to drug addictions are calmly considered as "lifestyle choices." Thus they are not something that society needs to be worried about. Yet, at a meeting of Alcoholics Anonymous, a speaker said, "No one chooses to be a helpless alcoholic."

And how about shelf labels in bookstores and video shops that classify pornographic books and videos as "adult" literature and movies? Doesn't that strike you as an insulting idea of what it is to be an adult in our society?

The choice of words manipulates reality and often generates nothing but confusion. The ongoing debate about abortion is not helped by the vocabulary each side selects. The pro-abortion community says the womb carries a fetus. The pro-life advocates say what is in the womb is a baby. Completely different perceptions of reality are wrapped up in those words.

A lot depends on the words we use. Which explains why spin doctors and people who want to promote a social or political agenda spend so much time picking and manipulating words.

It is not a new problem. You may remember the exchange Alice had with Humpty Dumpty.

"When I use a word," Humpty Dumpty said, in a rather scornful tone, "It means just what I choose it to mean — neither more nor less."

"The question is," said Alice, "whether you can make words mean so many different things."

"The question is," said Humpty Dumpty, "which is to be master — that's all."

The truth is, while sticks and stones may break our bones, it is words that can really hurt us.

PART TWO
TAKING CHARGE

TOGETHER WE STAND

I'm a great admirer of Sir Winston Churchill. In the war years, with my parents, I listened to his powerful speeches broadcast over the radio. Many of his words are permanently etched in my memory, as well in the record of the history of the Second World War. When Britain stood alone against the enemy, he said: "*We shall defend our island, whatever the cost may be, we shall fight on the beaches, we shall fight on the landing grounds ... we shall never surrender.*"

After the great air battles that beat back the enemy's aerial assault, he honoured the pilots: "*Never in the field of human conflict was so much owed by so many to so few.*"

And in his memorable words to our Parliament in Ottawa in December 1941, he said: "*When I warned them [the French government] that Britain would fight on alone whatever they did, their generals told their Prime Minister and his divided Cabinet: 'In three weeks England will have her neck wrung like a chicken.' Some chicken! Some neck!*"

For those who were moved by his words, who admired his

wartime leadership, he was proof positive of the Great Man theory of history. The idea is that, when push comes to shove, the course of history is driven by dynamic individuals who rise up to lead in times of distress, crisis, and need. The capital cities of the world are filled with statues, monuments, streets, and squares celebrating the leadership of kings, presidents, prime ministers, and generals credited with creating days of power and glory. "Those were the days, my friend. We thought they'd never end," went the words of a song popular about such heady times.

The question is frequently asked, why can't we have leaders like we had then, ones who were giants?

Given that deep-seated understanding of history, it is no mystery that so many are looking for a new Great Man to appear. The pressure is on political parties, nations, corporations, and institutions to pick star candidates to do the jobs that need to be done, meet the crises, save the nation and businesses, and stride steadfastly and confidently into the unknown future. No wonder so many candidates for leadership feel obliged to convince voters or shareholders that they alone can forge the road to glory.

Have you noticed that, when candidates are selected to lead political parties or to be mayors, their acceptance speeches usually include two themes?

First, they pour out gratitude to their family, their friends, and their campaign workers: all the foot soldiers who worked so hard for their selection as leader. "I could not have done it without you," they say.

Then, almost without taking a breath, the focus reverses. When *I* take office *I'll* fix things, *I'll* make changes, *I'll* bring prosperity and move the agenda forward, they say. And the people cheer; they have won, the job's done. Sadly, there is an inherent contradiction in the performance and in the situation. The people need a leader, but a leader needs the people. When a leader is chosen, the work has yet to begin.

In examining Churchill's leadership, it became clear to me how the Great Man theory of history is flawed. There can be little doubt that Churchill was a great man, a man of vision, courage, and stamina. Yet the essence of his leadership was in his ability to rally the British people. In the darkest days, he challenged them to accept hardships and strive for great achievements: "*Let us therefore brace ourselves to our duties, and so bear ourselves that, if the British Empire and its Commonwealth last for a thousand years, men will say, 'This was their finest hour.'* " And thus, in 1945, when peace came, he gave the people the credit for the victory. He said: "*I was not the lion, but it fell to me to give the lion's roar.*"

Leaders must be one side of a partnership such as president and people, CEO and workers, general and soldiers, captain and crew, or coach and team. It is to our own peril if we believe we can give responsibility to any one person. It is the source of tragedy and failure, the soil in which egomaniacs and tyrants prosper, the place where good leaders find themselves helpless and broken by burdens too great to carry alone.

We must stand together.

WHY THE OLIVE BRANCH?

We paused at a lookout on a mountain road in Greece that climbed from the Adriatic on the way to Delphi, where the oracles once delivered cryptic predictions of future events. As we looked down through the midday haze, we saw that the valley we'd just driven through was an endless olive-green carpet of trees.

"There must be a million olive trees down there!" someone said.

"Oh yes, more than a million," our Greek tour guide replied. "Some of them are over five hundred years old."

I'm sure that's true. Well-cared-for olive trees produce crops for generations and generations. Olive trees on the Mount of Olives, outside Jerusalem, are said to be close to two thousand years old.

Over the years, as old branches and trunks disintegrate, they are removed to nurture the shoots that spring from the roots and bark. Interestingly, it is nearly impossible to grow olive trees by planting olives. The way to grow a new tree is to root healthy branches and plant them, which is probably far more information than you ever wanted to know about olive trees.

I got curious about olive trees because I wondered why, from the most ancient times, antagonists seeking peace, or people promoting peace, speak of offering an olive branch to their enemy. Why, to this day, is the dove of peace drawn carrying a tiny olive branch in its beak? Why not a grapevine, a palm leaf, or a stalk of wheat? What is it about an olive branch that makes it so appropriate as a symbol of peace?

I assumed the answer would be about some Greek or Roman god. Or maybe the idea went back to the ancient Egyptians or Babylonians. I was wrong.

Olive branches are used as a symbol of peace because it takes from twelve to fifteen years after an olive branch is planted for it to produce any fruit. That's a long time. Planting olive trees is an investment in the future. Without the prospect of prolonged peace, no one plants them. Before planting, farmers want to be confident that they, or their sons and daughters, will live to see the harvest. So, offering an olive branch says you are committed to peace, big time.

Edward Gibbon, the historian who wrote about the decline and fall of the Roman Empire, said that, in the Empire, olive trees followed the progress of peace. They must have had a long time of peace in that Greek valley near the Gulf of Corinth.

It seems that when there is a conflict and war rages hot and heavy, the antagonists concentrate with so much intensity on survival, victory, and the sacrifices required to win that they often give little thought to what should happen after the conflict ends — to what is required to build peace.

Peace is having the confidence to plant trees that need fifteen years before they can bear fruit.

Peace is about knowing your children have lots of years to grow up in safety.

Peace is having time, even decades, for old wounds to heal and grim memories to fade.

Peace is about having the time to allow social structures in communities to arise and mature. And peace is about having the time to mend bridges, roads, houses, farms, and economies — about being able to hope.

Olive branches are reminders that there is no quick fix, there are no shortcuts.

It is encouraging to know there have been times when those simple truths were understood. Following the Second World War, the victorious Allies did not want to repeat the mistakes made after the First World War when the victors, crushed by the heavy price they had to pay for victory, demanded reparations from their enemies, leaving the defeated with new wounds that festered further over the years.

At the end of the Second World War, Europe was flooded with displaced people, great cities were piles of rubble, and governments and basic social institutions were shattered or nonexistent. Two great Americans, President Harry S. Truman and General George C. Marshall, understood that peace needed to be built, that peace needed time, needed nurturing. They established the Marshall Plan, a program of massive economic help that would allow a new Europe to emerge.

The plan was to help the people of Europe build a long-lasting peace and to make an end to their long history of warfare. Out of the ruins, a vibrant new Europe arose. In 1953, General Marshall was deservedly awarded the Nobel Peace Prize, the only general ever to be so honoured.

It takes a great general to know how to win a war and a greater one to know how to make peace.

THE GREATEST CHALLENGE

Everyone had been waiting for months. Finally, the hydro crew went from pole to pole turning the switches, and power flowed into the hamlets of Clyde Forks and Flower Station, just north of Lanark. In the summer of 1952, these were among the last places in rural Ontario to be connected to the province's power grid.

The lights went on, the fridges hummed, the toasters toasted, the radios sprang to life, electric kettles steamed, and electric saws, drills, and sewing machines were tested. Water flowed out of the taps, and marvellous ice cubes were made. It was like ten Christmases jammed into one day.

That night, I parked my motorcycle on a hill and looked back at the community of Clyde Forks. The lights flickered as people went from room to room to see each one with the new lights on. It was a magnificent day, a day that changed everything.

Energy changes things. The modern world has been created, enriched, and defined by its use of energy, from steam to nuclear power. The dominant, consistent ingredient in industrial and social progress has been the use of energy. The modern world — its strength, its civilization, its prosperity — has been linked to the availability and use of energy. Turn off the electricity, close the refineries, and the intricate structure of the modern world would quickly disintegrate.

We use power to communicate, to make goods, to transport people and things, and to produce our food. The people in another era, who talked about King Coal, understood that energy is the giant at the table.

In the developed world, we are concerned because we have seen our use of energy increase year after year. In the part of Oakville where I live, the local hydro company is replacing the underground wiring. Nothing is broken. It is just that a system installed thirty-five years ago doesn't meet our needs today — all the computers, dishwashers, air-conditioners, mixers, garage door openers, microwave ovens, and power tools we have plugged in.

In a world that relies on power, we are facing important questions about the sustainability of the supply of energy, about pollution, conservation, efficiency, and alternative sources. The spectre of the effects of global warming is frightening. The word is out that, if we put our efforts into harnessing wind, waves, and sun, and work seriously at conservation and efficiency, we'll be okay. There is talk that ten percent of the power we use today could be supplied by "green energy."

Sounds good. We should do all those things. However, there are a few problems.

Evidence shows that the amount of energy we need to sustain the fabric of our society grows faster than can be met by harvesting energy from wind, waves, water, and sun and conserving energy. By the time green energy meets today's ten percent estimate, our need for energy will have grown.

What about the underdeveloped countries? A graph plotting the levels of energy consumption per capita and the prosperity of people — their access to clean water, schools, medicine, food, and jobs — showed that energy consumption and social development followed the same line on the graph.

Lifting poor countries out of their poverty depends on their access to power. A huge amount of energy is needed because there are a lot of poor people and poor countries. This goes a long way toward explaining why developing countries with pollution problems are in no rush to sign accords to reduce or restrict their energy use.

Does that mean we are in a Catch-22 position?

Hardly. To begin, we need to stop talking about "less" and start talking about "more." The world needs more energy, not less. It is clear that to meet increased need, energy will have to come from technology that doesn't pollute or cause global warming.

What will the new sources be? I don't know. What we need is a giant international scientific energy research project. A twenty-first-century equivalent to the wartime Manhattan project to develop atomic energy or the massive effort to explore space. Yes, and add to that the size of the worldwide project to map the human genetic code.

It'll take at least a couple of decades to deal with this gigantic challenge. It is the greatest challenge the world has ever faced. It is time we got on with it.

THE FINAL FRONTIER

Telescopes located in space — the Hubble, Kepler, and Hipparcos — provide us with dramatic images of new stars, solar systems, galaxies, and, recently, a host of planets circling distant stars. There seems to be no end of cosmic wonders to behold. The more information gathered about the cosmos and the more mysteries solved, the more questions we have. Seeking answers, exploring, is one of the enduring characteristics of being human.

Finding these planets has renewed speculation about life on other planets, the possibility of visiting them, setting up colonies, and the chance that aliens could visit Earth.

Concerning the newly found planets, an astronomer at the University of Toronto said, "Mars is so much yesterday when we wonder about life as we know it on other planets. That twinkling pinpoint in the night could be an identical twin to Earth — and all we need are rocket ships that travel at the speed of light to get there for colonization."

I suspect he was testing the reporter's credulity. Surely he wasn't serious.

Those twinkling lights are light years away. A light year measures distances in space. One light year is the distance a beam of light travels in space in a year: That's 5.88 trillion miles. A trillion, as you know, is one followed by twelve zeros. (Big numbers like that give me a headache.) A small number is eight minutes, which is about how long it takes for sunlight to travel the ninety-three million miles to Earth.

So, how long would it take us to travel to the galaxy where the astronomers have spotted those new planets? At speeds at which we could *conceivably* travel, about three hundred thousand years. That's right, years! As a *New York Times* editorial said, that's a lot of time to be asking, "When will we get there?" How about the U of T astronomer's tongue-in-cheek, speed-of-light rocket ships? Ignoring the fact that going that fast is impossible, it would still take two thousand years to take a one-way trip to the planets discovered through the Kepler telescope.

Are we earthlings going to be able to visit other planets? Or can beings from other planets drop by here for a visit? In spite of the popularity of the TV series *Star Trek* and all the movies about battles with aliens out to conquer Earth, the answer is no. Stories about space travellers flipping from galaxy to galaxy, finding other civilizations and cultures, are pure fiction. But who said stories should obey the laws of physics?

I suspect our fascination with what is out there — challenging the Final Frontier — is driven, for many complex reasons, by our resistance to the idea that we may be unique creatures on a unique planet in the cosmos. But people used to believe that.

The early scientists — Copernicus, Kepler, Descartes, Galileo, Newton — proved that Earth was not the centre of the universe. As the years passed, it seemed to follow that the human race did not hold a special place in creation, that we are insignificant specks on a tiny planet circling a minor star in an obscure corner of the Milky Way galaxy.

Finding life on other planets would confirm that idea. It is part of who we are to want to "go where no one has gone before." Gathering information from out there is fascinating; we should never stop doing so.

Yet, as far as we know, after generations of study, the evidence is that our planet — and those who live on it — *are* special and unique. And given the evidence, the best working assumption is that we are alone, that we are the only ones who can build telescopes to probe the heavens, measure the depth of space, and ponder the very existence of the universe. We alone can create social structures that multiply individual efforts. We alone remember, tell stories, and dream of what might be. We are not insignificant specks. Our Earth is not just the third rock from the sun but the source of life.

If we can accept that, then our greatest challenge, our best bet to ensure the future, is to look after our own planet and one another. We won't find another place.

You have often heard the comment, "It's not rocket science," when the conversation turns to social issues: feeding the hungry, inoculating everyone from disease, giving education to all people, ensuring human rights, or stopping violence and oppression. The truth is, rocket science is complex and costly, but it's easy. That is, it's easy in comparison with building a peaceful world, feeding the hungry, building equality, and saving and healing the planet — our only home. To accomplish these things is to "go where no one has gone before."

The Final Frontier is not out there, light years away, but here, on this unique place called Earth.

GOODBYE GRIDLOCK

About thirty years ago, the term "gridlock" was coined to describe a traffic mess in New York City following a tunnel blockage. Today, congestion and gridlock are normal on our highways and byways. It is increasingly difficult to travel around in the Greater Toronto Hamilton Area (GTHA). The Toronto Board of Trade says: "… Gridlock and congestion impede our mobility and productivity … Toronto's lack of transportation infrastructure is a leading drag on our region's global competitiveness … Gridlock costs the region $6 billion annually." We are vying for the world record for the longest commute times to and from work.

None of this is news to "stop and go commuters," nor to those waiting for a bus on a cold winter evening, nor to those struggling to maintain a little personal space in crowded stations and transit vehicles.

There are, according to news reports and photo-ops, no end of plans and promises about subways, LRTs, better buses, and transit integration schemes. And so we hear regular announcements of billions for transit — particularly when elections are in the offing — as one level of government or another shows us diagrams, charts, and artistic renditions of modern trains and buses. Some improvements are made and some new vehicles are ordered; however, congestion and gridlock remain, because what gets done barely covers the need created by population increases in the GTHA.

With much trepidation — hopefully or foolishly — I toss a couple of suggestions into the debate.

A basic rule of life is: *Things are fixed sooner and better by the people who need them fixed.* With transit, that's us. Until now, we in the GTHA have looked to the provincial and federal governments to fix transit problems. The reality is that our transit needs are low on their agendas, which are already filled with the problems of health care, education, poverty, foreign affairs, national security, equipping the military, and the judicial system.

So the first step is: We need to get public transit out of the cabinet rooms and into our own hands. It is time we stopped asking *them* to fix things. It is *our* problem; *we* should take it over. A well-funded transit commission, with representatives from those who use the system, could be instituted, probably built on the existing Metrolinx group, moving from planning to management of transit in the GTHA.

Okay, you are right. There's an elephant in the room. It's that *well-funded* bit. How can we get the money? Do we penalize those driving cars by high parking costs, road tolls, and more tax on fuel? Or, as in London, impose a congestion charge to enter the core of the city? Most of these measures make it harder for ordinary citizens to get around, not easier. Which sort of defeats the purpose.

The Toronto Board of Trade, inadvertently perhaps, provides the answer. They have said that when a transit works well, every business and every employer benefits and that a well-run transit system is essential to the region's prosperity.

Here's how to find the money. Everyone, absolutely everyone, employed by business, government, and non-profit organizations, at every pay level, should, by law, receive a Monthly Transit Pass from their employer. By that simple measure, the way to build an effective transit system and the prosperity desired by the Board would be set in motion, all for about $120 a month per employee. Total cost, probably $2 billion a year: a bargain when congestion costs $6 billion and a good investment when employees and customers can come and go and do their business easily. It is not an untested idea. Every employee in Paris gets a transit pass for their efficient Metro. We'd need government help to give passes to students and help small businesses with the cost.

It wouldn't be easy to fit all the parts and pieces together and work with the many vested interests. Yes, we'd need a phase-in period (two to four years) to undertake new construction and get new equipment. The money issues during transition would be complex; we love to make money complicated.

Sure, there are lots of questions and many people need to help in finding answers. How can such a plan get underway? Well, a lot of the members of the Toronto Board of Trade could decide to give transit passes to all their employees. That would surely point the way ahead and get things moving.

They could call their plan Goodbye Gridlock.

FAMILY FIRE TRAPS

As long as I can remember, I've known about spontaneous combustion: how fires can start without — as the firemen put it — any external accelerant. A pile of oily rags and trash in a corner, a mound of wood chips warmed by the sun … Put almost any sort of flammable material under pressure and heat and a fire can start. That's why fire prevention inspectors tell us to clean up our basements and garages.

Which brings me to Katharine Hepburn. Yes, *that* Katharine Hepburn, the one who won all those Oscars and awards for her work in movies and on the stage. After living for a while in Los Angeles, Katharine escaped to the East Coast to a brownstone house at East 49th and 2nd Avenue in New York City. She ran away from being caught in spontaneous combustion.

Katharine Hepburn saw that the Hollywood lifestyle — with its mix of ego, ambition, competition, wealth, alcohol, drugs, sexual temptation, and the lure of fame — created all the conditions for disastrous relationships: conflagrations that consume and destroy people.

She wondered why so many stars and celebrities seemed surprised when their lives became a shambles, why they didn't recognize the elements for disaster swirling around them. It is still happening.

Today, the same atmosphere breeds a stream of serial marriages, breakups, and disasters in the lives of the rich and famous. It is all rich fodder for the jokes of late-night talk hosts such as Leno and Letterman.

The size of the destructive lifestyle is demonstrated when Jay or David reveals that a celebrity guest has been married for twenty or twenty-five years. The audience applauds as enthusiastically as if the guest had won an Olympic Medal. Maybe they do deserve the applause (after all, we should reward success) for not being consumed by a society seething with the destructive elements and forces that destroy so many.

As comedians, tabloids, fan magazines, and TV shows track the lives of celebrities and capitalize on the latest breakdown or breakup, they miss important issues. Celebrities are people, too, and there is a high cost to be paid as they cope with dashed hopes and face struggles to heal their wounds and to get their lives glued back together. To profit from their pain seems macabre.

It should also be noted that spontaneous combustion in human relationships is not confined to the communities of the rich and famous. Therapists and counsellors, to help their clients, often spend a lot of time looking for smouldering piles of stuff dumped in the corners. These are the untidy crannies in our heads stuffed with bits and pieces of unresolved anger, injustices we've endured (real or perceived), things we've never forgotten or forgiven that were done to us or we did to ourselves.

It is a combustible pile that can burst, without warning, into flame under the slightest increase in pressure or heat in our lives. It doesn't take much, as we might so aptly observe afterwards, because "it was the last straw."

Doing a bit of tidying up and dealing with the accumulation before these things catch fire and spoil the present would seem to be a good idea. "An ounce of prevention is worth a pound of cure."

Spontaneous combustion also takes place out there in the world, in high-risk places, situations, and lifestyles. To the age-old fire traps of alcohol, drugs, and sex have been added the heat and pressure of hedonism, prosperity, and fashion; the easy anonymity in far-off places; legalized gambling; the idea that self-fulfillment trumps commitments.

How many of these things can a person get into before there's spontaneous combustion? No one can say. Too many seem bound to test themselves to the flashpoint, and then, far too often, it is too late.

Life's survival manual, honed by thousands of years of hard-won experience, gives this advice: "Head for the exits." Get out of there. Run for your life. Eliminate, or at least reduce, the heat and pressure. Following that simple advice can save a life.

It can save yours.

CHECKING BAGGAGE

I've been lucky enough to travel and see places I'd never dreamed of visiting. I've even got used to long flights and waiting in airports, although it'll take a while before I'll be easy with the intense security checks these days.

My problem with travelling is packing. It's the business of figuring out what to take "in case" it is cold, hot, rainy, or all of them on the same day. I never get it right. I forget important stuff and take things I never wear. I've gone on a long trip without pyjamas and, one time at a fancy hotel, while getting ready to go out for dinner, discovered that the dress shoes I'd packed consisted of a brown left shoe and a black right shoe.

And there's the "what if" stuff: what you'll need if there's an unexpected opportunity to attend a special event. I mean, you never know, maybe invitations will surface to meet some dignitary or to go to Buckingham Palace.

I know I should travel light, with a small bag. It probably won't happen soon. At least I don't pack for the palace. If the Queen invites me, I'll buy or rent the appropriate stuff.

It's a relief when my bag, all tagged, jiggles its way out of sight on the airport conveyor belt. It's out of my hands. I can't add or remove anything. I can sit content in the departure lounge with my fellow passengers.

Departure lounges these days are filled with fascinating people of all sizes and shades of skin and wearing everything from serious suits to loose pyjama-like outfits apparently rescued from old gym bags.

There's a man nervously checking his pockets for his passport, ticket, and boarding pass, each time adding to his anxiety by shifting them to a "better" pocket. Sitting across from him, a woman, who has asked at least four people if this is the right gate, gets up to check once more, this time with the gate attendant, who has just appeared.

Also in the departure area is a young woman nervously flipping a textbook's pages, highlighted and tabbed with Post-it notes. She's not reading, just going through the motions. Close by, a thin, angular man is surrounded by a cluster of cloth, plastic, and paper bags: treasures he daren't entrust to the airline or let out of his sight in this world of thieves.

There's a confrontation at the gate. A man, his face red with anger, waves his ticket and boarding pass in the attendant's face, as he tells her what he thinks of the system and the airline.

Looking around, it is clear that, in spite of our care in packing, most of us set out on our journey — and on our travels through life — carrying baggage we can't leave at the check-in counter or in closets at home. We bring anger, tension, anxiety, fear, and other habits with us. It is the sort of baggage that will have a huge influence on whether we have a good holiday or a successful business trip and will govern how we react to the unknown and unexpected.

I suspect all of us lug this kind of baggage around day after day like an invisible backpack we put on as we awake each morning. Why don't we pack up the negative stuff, like anxiety and fear, and dump it?

It's because we have been led to believe we can't be anything other than what we are. Popular wisdom today tells us that our character — who we are — is determined by our genes, by the early years of our lives, the environment we live in, and even by the year of our birth. As we can't change any of that, we are stuck with who we are. Nothing can be done.

Well, to believe that is to believe a big thing! If our lives are determined by such things, if we are not free to choose what we do or what we'll be, then ultimately we are not responsible for anything. If that is so, we are to be pitied.

Of course, it is nonsense. We know we have choices to make. We know old habits can be broken and new and better ones learned. We can do better. After all, I've trained myself not to keep checking my documents in the departure lounge.

THE DA VINCI FLAW

Leonardo da Vinci was a genius. He was a painter, sculptor, architect, scientist, mathematician, engineer, inventor, anatomist, musician, and writer. His journals and notebooks — full of notations on building bridges, flying machines, catapults, fortifications, harbours, and canals and with accurate anatomical drawings of humans and animals — are a testimony to his genius.

However, in his last days, he said, "I have wasted my life."

How could that be? Well, he had a tragic flaw. He never managed to concentrate his genius or his skills. He was easily distracted. He left paintings unfinished and was easily bored with the tedious work of testing his ideas, theories, and insights. Leonardo was known in his day as a great procrastinator, always claiming he'd get back to things.

Leonardo's flaw is not unique. There are many stories of brilliant people — polymaths with huge potential — who didn't do well. That's true enough, but the da Vinci Flaw is not peculiar to geniuses. It is a common condition found in both young and old who are sure they have missed their chances or made a mess of life.

In the middle of the first decade of this century, a newspaper report looked at the situation of people turning thirty. Many of those interviewed said they had wasted their lives. All their great expectations about where they'd be when they turned thirty were unfulfilled. They had gone from one thing to another, from job to job, from interest to interest, purposefully not getting involved with commitments, leaving themselves free and open, waiting for life to unfold. Many had returned to the comfort of their parents' home, back to the old bedroom, to the recreation room with the stereo and Nirvana poster.

Dumbledore, head of Hogwarts — the school for wizards that Harry Potter went to — told Harry, "The course of life is not determined by the talents you were given but by the choices you make." That's good advice for a young wizard becoming aware of his powers and of the expectations people have of him. They are wise words for all of us.

Life is about making choices. Not just about the cheese you should buy or which Starbucks coffee you will order, but about what you are going to do with your life, with the time you have on Earth.

To say life is about choices seems so obvious it ought to be left in the category of things that go without saying. However, to many, the process of making choices is not all that simple or clear.

Here's the rub: What it means is that you can't have it all. Having it all is apparently what many people are about. They multi-task, they are connected 24/7, they dash from one thing to another, squeezing their schedules, rushing to fit in the job, family, golf, mini-vacations, working lunches, and so forth. And some are proud of the way they handle "fly in, fly out" airport meetings. Their lives are so hectic, they can't find any time to figure out what "having it all" means.

What is "all" and how do you know when you have enough of it? The sorry plight of many so-called celebrities these days probably arises because they've never reflected on that question.

The way choices work is that every yes you say requires you to say no, and to say it a lot of times. "No" is the important word on the road to accomplishment. The commitment and practice time required to be a competitive hockey player or swimmer means you can't be both. To pass an apprenticeship course or rise up in a job or profession means you must say no to a lot of attractive alternatives.

Biographies of successful people often reveal that, at some point in their lives, they selected a major goal for themselves: to make a difference in their community; to make a contribution through their work to society; to raise independent children; or to uphold honourable standards. Life seems to work best when goals are substantial and challenging and reach beyond the narrow confines of one's life and benefit.

Marcus Aurelius, an Emperor of Rome and a philosopher, wrote: "Guard against … the folly of those who weary their days in much business but lack any aim on which their whole effort, nay, their whole thought is focused."

Leonardo probably never got around to reading those words.

BLAMING THE VICTIMS

Public service spots on TV show compulsive gamblers explaining that they never planned to lose everything. They can't believe it happened to them. Well, obviously, ending up beaten and broken is no one's goal in life. Still, gambling, drinking, trying drugs, smoking, pornography, and overeating — all the wide variety of addictions and vices — wreak havoc and destroy many lives.

The idea that fully one-third of university students would succumb to vices and addictions, one-third would lack ability, and only one-third would graduate was predicted by Otto von Bismarck, the chancellor of Germany, in the late nineteenth century. In 1950, the president of Carleton University quoted Bismarck's words to the incoming students. The prediction proved to be accurate when the graduates marched in their gowns to receive their degrees.

I have no idea about the percentage of people broken by addictions in our twenty-first century, but it has to be substantial. There are twelve-step programs, such as Alcoholics Anonymous, to help victims who are struggling with a wide variety of addictions. Even so, a recent newspaper article reported that alcoholism in Canada kills more people than diseases like AIDS and heart disease.

Step number one in these programs is for the person to accept responsibility for their addiction. Before a group, members have to own up to their bad choices and their lack of self-control and willpower. Accepting responsibility is the essential first step in the healing process.

However, the willingness of the addicted to shoulder all the blame, though essential in the healing process, may actually distort the reality. Maybe the fault does not rest completely on the shoulders of the victims. Could it be the problem is not simply about a lack of willpower?

In all honesty, we must take into account the presence in our society of a vast army of people, commanding huge resources, who are dedicated to promoting destructive, addictive lifestyles: lotteries, casinos, and online poker; alcohol in all its various manifestations; overeating; and the infusion of sexual exploitation into the heart of our culture. We live in a time when some of the smartest people around spend their lives figuring out ways to defeat our self-control.

Professor Kathleen Vohs of the University of Minnesota recently wrote, "There is research that shows people still have the same self-control as in decades past, but we are bombarded more and more with temptation [and] our psychological system is not set to deal with all the potential immediate gratification."

Should we ignore the influence of the culture of temptation and continue to lay all the blame on those who become victims?

Are they solely responsible for what befalls them? In other times, places, and societies, many customs and social structures supported and encouraged people to exercise their willpower in avoiding the traps and pitfalls on life's torturous journey.

We tend to vastly overrate our ability to exercise self-control and resist temptation. Professor Loran Nordgren of the Kellogg School of Management recently said, "The people who are most self-confident also, as a result, expose themselves to more temptation than others, which also makes them most likely to fail." Indeed, there are many situations in which having willpower and resisting temptation are considered anti-social.

The key strategy in supporting your self-control is to control your environment. If you want to lose weight, don't have dishes of peanuts on the table or go to an all-you-can-eat buffet restaurant. Want to cut out alcohol? Keep away from bars. Casinos are a bad scene if you need to control your gambling. If you want to be faithful in marriage, don't trust your self-control: Head for the nearest exit when you feel the first hint of attraction to someone else.

So the basic strategy — to avoid being among the one-third of those who succumb to temptation — is to work on environmental control. That is a very hard truth. Far too many, young and old, assume it is a sign of weakness not to try everything, to go everywhere, or to play in dangerous places.

Think about it: Controlling your environment is a simple strategy. It works.

HOW TO GET A LIFE

I've been trying to figure out what it means when someone says "get a life." Does it mean get with the latest fad or addiction? Should one throw all restraint aside? Stop relying on others? Trust the maxim that you can be whatever you want? Take charge of your own life?

It is hard to know. The idea that you can be whatever you want drives our society. It is what we tell young people in order to inspire them to hold bold expectations. It sounds good, but young people soon see that it isn't so.

One of the stellar comic skits of all time featured Dudley Moore and Peter Cook of *Beyond the Fringe*, an old TV program from England. Moore plays a one-legged man named Spiggott, who, hopping on one leg, applies to Cook to play the part of Tarzan.

Cook: "Well, Mr Spiggott, need I point out to you where your deficiency lies as regards landing the role?"

Moore: "Yes, I think you ought to."

Cook: "Need I say, without overmuch emphasis, that it is in the leg division that you are deficient?"

Moore: "The leg division?"

Cook: "Yes, the leg division, Mr Spiggott. You are deficient in it to the tune of one. Your right leg, I like. I like your right leg. A lovely leg for the role. That's what I said when I saw you come in. I said, 'A lovely leg for the role.' I've got nothing against your right leg. The trouble is — neither have you. You fall down on your left."

Moore: "You mean it's inadequate?"

Cook: "Yes, it's inadequate, Mr Spiggott. And to my mind, the British public is just not ready for the sight of a one-legged ape man swinging through the jungle tendrils."

As the skit points out, you need two legs to play Tarzan. You also need an astronomical IQ to be a genius and to be well over five foot four to play NBA basketball. Oh, and if you have a tin ear, don't even think about a career as an opera singer.

And, obviously, only one person can be Prime Minister of Canada, and only one person can be CEO of Microsoft, at any one time.

So, to tell someone "you can be anything you want" is to perpetuate a lie. Yet, there are elements imbedded in the saying that are true.

The first truth: To fulfill your potential in life requires dedication, hard work, and discipline. Without those qualities, people flounder around waiting for the fickle finger of fate to chart the course of their lives.

The late Ray Kroc, former CEO of McDonald's, often quoted the words of former U.S. president Calvin Coolidge: "Press on ... nothing in this world can take the place of persistence.

Talent will not; nothing is more common than unsuccessful people with talent. Genius will not; unrewarded genius is almost a proverb. Education will not; the world is full of educated derelicts. Persistence and determination alone are omnipotent." That's a message we all need.

The second truth: As we work on designing our lives, we need to be aware that hard work and persistence are not enough. The future is always heavily influenced by the values, principles, and ethics we hold, and by old-fashioned qualities like truth, honesty, integrity, faithfulness, and self-control.

Of course you know all that. In the 2001 movie *K-Pax*, Kevin Spacey played the part of Prot, who claimed he was from the distant planet K-Pax. Among other questions, he was asked what the moral laws were like on his planet.

"Every being in the universe knows right from wrong," he replied.

Knowing is good, living is better. It is how you determine whether you carry a burden of unresolved anger, of painful regrets, or carry a sense that you have done your best in your life in your part of the world.

And so we come to the third truth. You can make a life even if you only have one leg or lack the gifts to be an opera diva. As quoted earlier, Albus Dumbledore, head of Hogwarts School of Witchcraft and Wizardry, tells Harry Potter, "The course of life is not determined by the talents you were given, but by the choices you make." Which means we don't have to be wizards to get a life.

THE JOHN WAYNE MYTH

John Wayne, "The Duke," starred in a couple hundred films portraying rugged, individualistic heroes. It was a role he loved so much, he worked hard off-camera to emulate that persona in his everyday life. He occupies an important place in one of the most powerful myths around: the John Wayne myth.

What's that? It's the myth repeated over and over in books and movies. You know the story: A lone rider, a gunfighter, a maverick, one strong individual alone saves the ranch, the town, the mine, or the damsel in distress and turns certain defeat into victory.

John Wayne died nearly thirty years ago, but the John Wayne myth lives on. You see it played out in the hard edged TV series *24*. There, the indestructible Jack Bauer, played by Kiefer Sutherland, solves the most urgent and complex problems in twenty-four hours. He overcomes every daunting challenge as the clock ticks down the minutes and seconds left to defeat the bad guys. He is smarter, faster, and braver and is never slowed down by beatings or injuries. Crucial to his success is that he is a maverick, a loner, and outside the community.

Myths help us to define our dreams and our idea of what ought to be. The problem with the John Wayne myth is it leads us down wrong paths. In the back of our minds, there's a hope, a dream, maybe even an expectation that a hero will arise to slay the dragons, fix the problems, and save our society, like John Wayne riding into town to take charge.

It is the sort of vague notion that seems to be central to the way our democratic process appears to work. In each election we seem to be searching for a heroic leader who will fix everything that is wrong and slay the dragons. We vote for the person who convinces us that he or she will look after everything. Having voted, having done our democratic duty, we quickly get back to our lives, leaving all to the wonder worker. Sadly, the elected hero is probably unable to slay the dragons and produce wonders. Oops, wrong person! Well, next time we'll try again to find our heroine or hero … and thus the cycle goes on and on.

In the play *The Life of Galileo* by Bertolt Brecht, a character says to Galileo, "Unhappy the land that has no heroes!" To which Galileo replies, "No. Unhappy the land that needs heroes."

A huge part of the movie *Flags of Our Fathers*, about the U.S. Marine Corp's costly assault on Pacific island Iwo Jima in the Second World War, focuses on three men, survivors of the team who raised the U.S. flag on the island, an act captured in a photograph that is an enduring American symbol.

At the end of the battle, the three men were hustled back to the U.S. to be displayed as heroes at war bond rallies. They were deeply embarrassed; they hated the experience and insisted they were not heroes. The victory was won by all the men who went ashore — by all who died, were wounded, or survived. They were not John Wayne characters; they were regular guys.

Most people hailed as heroes don't like the title. Are they needlessly humble? No, it's just that they know they were just doing their jobs: what had to be done as part of the team, part of the unit's effort.

The story of the settlement of the American West and the Canadian West is the same story. It's about pioneers who opened the land, built schools, houses, shops, courthouses, and churches: people who looked after each other in times of trouble and harvest. (The only difference is that, in the U.S., there was a brief time of lawlessness, while we had the Mounties to keep the peace.) The settlers did not see themselves as heroes, but they did great things by working together. It is the way the world works.

We should stop looking for heroes and vote for leaders who can get people involved, working together, and looking after each other. To change the words of John F. Kennedy a bit, "Ask not what your leader can do for you, ask what we can do for each other."

THAT COULD HAVE BEEN ME

In the 1930s, two blocks from our house in Ottawa, were two vacant properties thick with trees. We kids knew them as the Big Bush and the Little Bush. Our parents warned us never to go past the signs that read "Trespassers Will Be Prosecuted." The warnings and signs, heightened by stories older kids told of their forays into the bushes, gave these areas an aura of delicious mystery and danger.

One of the marks of growing up, in our little corner of the world, was to venture into the Big Bush. It was midway through a summer afternoon when Eddie and I ventured along a well-worn path. The Big Bush seemed dark in the shadow of the trees. The path went this way and that … then ahead it was brighter. We stepped into a clearing.

We stared at a pile of ashes and at sticks to hold pots over a fire. Hanging on the trees were pots, a coat, and a sweater, and near the fire was a log seat, beside it a carefully folded newspaper. We hurried out along the path. Wow! We had passed; we had a story to tell. We'd warn the little kids.

We had discovered a hobo camp. It was empty because the men were out seeking work or collecting food: something for the pots hanging on the tree. At that time in Canada, there were thousands and thousands of men like them and a host of destitute families.

They relied on charity: a sandwich, a bowl of soup, a coffee. They wore second-hand shoes and clothes and hoped to be given a dime, maybe even a quarter. It took a great outpouring of generosity and compassion by individuals, charities, and churches to barely sustain these victims of the Great Depression.

Those who had little shared what little they had. People said, "There, but for the grace of God, go I." They knew there was a fine line between any of us and tragedy or destitution.

Whatever became of the men from the camp? Probably some were among the first to sign up when war broke out in 1939. Later, as the war wound down, they joined those who had helped press the government to take responsibility for our country's unfortunates. It was wrong to leave the task of meeting people's basic needs for food, shelter, and clothing to charity alone.

Canadians demanded that compassion be high on the agenda of the nation. Thus, starting in the 1940s and '50s, we saw acts passed to provide old age pensions, the baby bonus, unemployment insurance, and government-financed rental housing all across Canada. In time, the Canada Health Act was passed. We were proud of our social safety net.

Yet, once again, charities are facing a crushing struggle to meet the desperate needs of our people. Today, there are huge holes in the safety net. Under the bridges and overpasses, ragged collections of the homeless try to establish communities.

What started as emergency responses to needs — food banks, clothing depots, Out of the Cold shelter programs, and winter night patrols to provide blankets, coats, mitts, and hot soup to street people — are becoming permanent tasks.

The charities are terrific in dealing with emergencies. Involved, person-to-person, they're sensitive to the pain and suffering of the homeless, the hungry, the sick, and all who live on the edge of despair.

There, in the trenches, they react to emergencies faster than governments can. These days, homelessness, hunger, and poverty are beyond being an emergency. Food drives that once provided extra food for Christmas now have to be run all year long.

The problems are endemic. Only governments can fix the basic inequalities and the problems plaguing our cities and towns.

How can we have such need in these prosperous days? We could easily lose our way in a maze of complex explanations. Action is needed. Those who survived the 1930s had a plan. It worked.

First, remember that bad times can come to anyone. "There, but for the grace of God, go I." Then, lean hard on the politicians to deal with the problems, heal the wounds, end the hunger, and shelter the homeless.

It's time to fix the net, to reaffirm the compassion that defines us as Canadians.

OVER THE LINE

After the Napoleonic wars, the British Navy took on the responsibility of keeping the seas open for world trade. Ships plied the world's seas to earn huge profits for merchants and ship owners. However, the bell at Lloyd's, the insurer of ships, tolled far too often announcing the loss of ships and crews. To manage the risky business and protect their profits, ship owners had the voyages well insured. The loss of ships and crews was considered normal: the result of the traditional dangers faced by those who go down to the sea in ships.

Some knew that was nonsense. The ships that went down were so overloaded, there was no margin of safety. Moderately bad winds or high seas easily overwhelmed those ships.

Samuel Plimsoll, a British MP, led a campaign in Parliament against overloading and over-insuring ships. His plan was to paint a maximum load line on the sides of all merchant ships. A bill to that end was presented to Parliament in 1875. Furious opposition from ship owners, traders, and industrialists — who claimed they would be ruined — forced the government to withdraw the bill.

Plimsoll, with those who supported the law, appealed to the public to help them eliminate the coffin ships. It worked. The next year, the bill was reintroduced and passed. From that time, every merchant ship has a load line on its hull. It is called the Plimsoll Line.

Interesting trivia, but what has it to do with today? Just this: We have a severe overload problem today in our marketplace and could use some kind of Plimsoll Line.

What is overloaded? The workers who are on call 24/7: the ones expected to do overtime day after day; who need to get to work early and leave late lest they seem disloyal; and who, on weekends and holidays, are expected to check their messages and e-mails. The army of people who regularly eat lunch at their keyboards; except, of course, when the boss schedules a working lunch.

Overloaded workers are so common, such a part of corporate culture, it has become "the new normal" way to do business. I hear that quite a large number of people have difficulty with taking holidays. They're afraid they'll lose out, get out of touch, may be passed over, or, at least, appear to be less than loyal team players.

When forced to take time off, they try to make sure they are not away for more than a week at a time. They also make sure to pack their communication devices, so they can log-on two or three times a day. You've probably seen advertisements for computers that feature pictures of people on cottage docks or on the beach working away on their laptops. No wonder the Internet providers are hustling to provide their service to resort and recreation areas.

There are no load-limits, no Plimsoll Lines for the workplace in these early years of the twenty-first century. Many work day after day at a maximum load factor and, like overloaded ships, there's no safety margin. With no wiggle room, it doesn't take much to be too much. All it takes to hit the breaking point is another call on the weekend, another extra assignment, an automatic expectation that you'll do overtime, a late-day conference call, the endless influx of e-mails, or perhaps a task that is not, by itself, huge or impossible but is the proverbial last straw.

The results are duly observed, and the casualty list is discussed quietly and nervously over coffee. Stress-related illnesses are on the increase. Workers try to cope with chronic frustration as they can't keep up and lack the time to do a proper job. As workers are worn down with frustration and anxiety, efficiency, productivity, and creativity in the workplace all slip lower and lower, and the number of sick days taken rises.

None of this is news. Self-help books and articles in business publications offer advice on how to deal with stress, how to handle workloads, how to keep up the pace, and how to be a survivor. Do you understand what they are saying? If you have a job these days — if you go down to the sea in ships — you must live with the risk of drowning. It is your problem. Those who reap in the profits, who run the businesses, have no problem, no responsibility.

Where is Samuel Plimsoll when we need him? We need someone like him to set limits, to draw lines. Of course, maybe too many are making money the way it is.

PREPARING TO FIGHT THE VIKINGS

Tomorrow no Viking raiders from the sea will appear through the dawn mists to ransack and plunder our homes. Tomorrow we do not need to carry Colt revolvers when we go out because there's a chance we'll have to fight for our lives before we are home again.

Our cities and towns do not need strong walls with gates we can lock at sundown. Unlike the citizens of ancient Rome, we do not need armed guards to travel with us at night. A poor harvest in our part of the country doesn't mean that famine and death will strike our family in the winter.

We are lucky people. Crime rates are falling year after year. Many of us have never met anyone who has been a victim of a violent crime. Our stores are filled with good food and all the necessities of life.

Conditions and diseases that our grandparents justly feared, such as scurvy, rickets, smallpox, polio, diphtheria, scarlet fever, and malnutrition, are mostly unknown to us. Our infant mortality rate is very low, and our life expectancy rises year after year.

And yet we live in a culture of fear.

There are a host of fear mongers out there who seem to have a vested interest in convincing us we are in imminent danger. A single report of an isolated case of a rare disease, or a news item about a dramatic crime, is enough to get the fear mongers going. Right on cue, special interest and advocacy groups grab the headlines as they predict dire futures on the basis of slim statistics.

Talk-show hosts on radio and TV, in the name of balanced coverage (and ratings), give the same amount of airtime to people with strange, far-out ideas as to those who have studied the issues for years.

Perhaps we should also take note of the fascination we have with bad news and the way movie and television producers play with violence, celebrate disasters, and delight in portraying the psychotic and the occult.

With the power of modern communications, fears can spread like wildfire.

At any rate, many are sure that it's a jungle out there, that our neighbourhood streets are unsafe, and that we are in danger from the candles we burn, the food we eat, and the air we breathe. Everything we buy comes labelled with warnings. It is easy to conclude that we teeter precariously on the edge of some disaster or another.

Our society seems to suffer from hypochondria.

As a result, we are a cautious people. We watch our children carefully to try to save them from every possible risk and danger. We bus and drive them everywhere. We watch them so well, they are seldom unsupervised, left alone to learn about risk, to measure their tree-climbing skills, or find a new way home from school. Maybe we're going too far?

For example, the Toronto School Board tore out millions of dollars worth of playground equipment the safety experts said were dangerous. Did you see any report from the board on how many children had been injured on the slides and swings? Some officials spoke of "zero tolerance for risk." I figure I learned a lot from skinned knees, broken bones, and being afraid.

Sure, our society is safe. We don't have to fight Vikings, but it is not risk-free. If you fall down, you get hurt. Lots of things are not good to do. There are bad people. Children need to know about such things; we all do.

And yet we have to be wary lest we allow fear to take control of what we do. Fear can drive us behind triple-locked doors. Fear can cause us to assume that every stranger, every place, is a threat until we are too afraid to go to ordinary places or do ordinary things.

The challenge of life is what it has always been. It is about becoming strong enough and wise enough to measure risk, handle danger, and deal with trouble. It's about being courageous in the face of threats and the unpredictable twists and turns of life.

We don't want our children to be foolhardy. But it is essential to teach them to be strong and wise, to face danger, troubles, and threats, and to be aware of the unpredictability of our existence. It is almost like preparing to fight the Vikings.

THE POWER OF ONE

Things seem pretty normal this year. Of course, normal means we have had a regular serving of natural disasters: floods, storms, forest fires, earthquakes, and volcanic eruptions. And we have had wars, accidents, tragedies, and enough evidence of malfeasance, chicanery, and incompetence to keep the newspapers and the solemn hosts of investigative TV programs busy.

It is all "normal" and "to be expected," the stuff of statistics — impersonal and understandable. That is, unless some of the stuff happens to us. Then it is hard to take.

Knowing about statistics and probabilities doesn't provide much comfort when the operating number is one. Statisticians can't deal with *one* as a number. They can figure things out when they have thousands and millions, but not with one. The laws of averages break down with the number one. That's understandable, but every statistic, in fact, is full of ones. You and I are ones. When you are the one who gets sick, has an accident, or gets downsized out of a job, it hardly seems normal. For most of us, normal means a life that is pretty routine with only minor irritations. The surprises are unexpected, as well as unpredictable.

It is hard living the unpredictable existence of a one. When things go wrong, it is natural to get angry and ask, "Why should this happen to me?" And it is natural to want to blame someone if we end up on the wrong side of the statistics. Finding someone to blame is a growth industry in our society.

Behind the blame business is the idea that society should be risk free. *They* should have known, *they* should have checked, *they* were negligent. Of course, there are a lot of things that need to be fixed, and the Peter Principle (which states people rise to their level of incompetence) has not been refuted. In the end, a simple fact remains: Life can never be risk free. Risk can be reduced, balanced, and taken, but never eliminated.

Living is a high-risk business. Physical and biological laws have never been repealed. If you fall down a flight of stairs, you are probably going to break something.

And yet, we have lowered the risks. We live longer lives, have better living conditions, better medical care, and better (and more) food than any other society since the first people walked this Earth and struggled to survive. How hard it must have been for them. Actually, we don't have to look that far back. The diseases and weaknesses caused by malnutrition were common even in the prosperous countries of the West only seventy or eighty years ago. We are doing pretty well.

Of course, saying that things were worse then, that we are fortunate, isn't terribly comforting when you have troubles and when your normal life is in disarray because you are on the wrong side of the statistics.

What is at stake is living and finding a way to cope and move forward.

A good strategy is to back away from any anger about the unfairness of it all. Fairness, equality, what is deserved, and what should be or ought to be — all of these things usually have absolutely nothing to do with what you have to deal with. As you only have so much energy, it is not wise to expend it in anger.

But what if it is not your fault? What if there *is* someone to blame: a culprit, a scapegoat, or an enemy? It is possible to be consumed with finding satisfaction, with revenge. If that course of action is taken, it exacts its toll: It consumes the present, poisons the future, and leaves behind pools of bitterness. You would be shocked to know how many people leave behind only vivid memories of their unsatisfied wrath.

How much better it is to act like an army after a battle. Count your resources; figure out what is left and what can be saved. Then, having assessed the situation, know what you can do with all that to make things better for you and for those you share your life with. It will probably reveal a lot more resources and possible courses of action than you expected you had.

After all, we are not cold statistics; we are people; we are *ones*. We are not easily slotted into categories. We can defy the odds.

THE SURVIVAL OF THE FITTEST

On the main road, our tour coach crossed a bridge spanning an incredibly deep ravine near Sorrento. The Romans built it two thousand years ago. After crossing the bridge, I wondered how many men it took to cut and move all that stone and how the Roman engineers organized it all.

But it is more than that. The very existence of that bridge is a serious challenge to people who are always saying things like "It's a dog-eat-dog world out there," "It's a rat race," "It's the survival of the fittest."

The phrase "the survival of the fittest" comes from Charles Darwin's work on the origin of species. It sums up his theory about how creatures with the best adaptations survive while those who don't adapt don't. It is a useful concept, for it helps us to understand our environment.

However, Darwin's insights have little to do with people or with our survival, success, or failure.

The human race opted out of biological determinism long, long ago.

It happened when our distant ancestors saw that, if they worked together, they would all benefit. One could keep watch at night, while others slept. They could build better shelters and get more to eat when they worked and hunted together.

The determining characteristic of humanity is not our biology, but our community.

Creating communities — sharing our skills and knowledge and combining our collective energy — ranks right up there with the invention of language and the discovery of fire as a huge leap forward for humanity. It may even top the list.

The invention of the community was a master step that broke our biological bonds. Working together freed us. It meant we could build bridges, dig canals, build boats, and create all sorts of things.

It has taken a lot of work, but we have managed pretty well. We invented councils, governments, and constitutions to help us live together and serve the common good. We devised courts to settle disputes without violence. We put together schools to pass on knowledge and skills. We have striven hard to work things out so people can do what they do best, like making flint arrowheads or designing nuclear reactors. We have created thousands of structures to organize ways to work, share, and help one another.

The human story is not about biological determinism: the survival of the fittest, a dog-eat-dog existence. To live on the level of the survival of the fittest means we have failed to be human. The human story is really a story about communities.

However, it is not easy getting community business done in

a society where individual rights have a high profile and priority. Our names are not posted on lists telling us of our regular turn on night watch or when to help dig the community well. It is not easy, in a money economy, to be sure where we fit in, or to know whether what we do matters.

And so, while a lot of us grumble about how things are run, we prefer to act on the assumption that things will roll along without our getting involved. It seems to be working. We happen to live in the country the UN says is the best in the world. And yet, we who live here know we have problems. Maybe all the UN is telling us is that others are worse off.

It's hard to be complacent when there are so many things that need improvement, so many problems to be worked out, so many agendas out of kilter, and so many people who are misused or excluded. Can things ever work perfectly when they're run by imperfect people?

Being complacent can be very dangerous. The very ancestors who invented communities learned the hard way that leaving the running of the community to "them" could lead to disaster. Things could easily get out of hand. Often the structures and the people who were meant to serve delivered, instead, suffering, enslavement, and chaos.

The community needs us. It is our business. It is our business to make sure we never fall into the mode of the survival of the fittest. It is the business of each of us to shoulder the burdens of building and running our community. The work begun by our ancestors never ends. It is the work that makes us part of humanity.

PRIMED AND LOADED

The mail brought a picture of me that was taken on a trip. I was fascinated by it. No, not by me with the standard grimace I get on my face when my picture is being taken. What interested me was everything else in the photo: the lovely flowers in the planter, the fancy brickwork in the building, the intricate iron railings in front of the windows, and, on the left side of the photo, a man with a pushcart filled with articles for sale.

It is certainly was me in the photo. Obviously I had been there. But I don't remember the flowers, the brickwork, or the man with the pushcart.

I missed it all because I wasn't paying attention. My mind was somewhere else, probably thinking about the next place we were going. Because of my anxiety about the next thing on the itinerary, I missed out on what was around me, what was happening. The coach leaves in fifteen minutes; better be there. It wasn't that I didn't "stop to smell the roses." I never even saw the roses, or whatever the flowers were.

So now when someone says we should stop and smell the

roses, I know they haven't really understood the problem. You have to see the roses first. You have to be present, conscious of your surroundings, rather than mostly concerned about where you'll be next or what the next problem, meeting, presentation, dinner, or weekend might hold for you. Missing the roses is only part of the problem.

Captains of warships, in the days of sail, sighting what might be an enemy ship in the distance, would order the ship cleared for action. On rare occasions, they would even order the gun crews to prime and load their cannons but leave the gun ports closed so as not to alert the potential enemy. As they sailed to meet the suspicious ship, tense sailors crouched behind the closed gun ports, ready on a second's notice to let loose a broadside. It was a dangerous tactic. One mistake, a misfire, would wreak havoc.

It seems when we live in advance, concentrating on what might or can happen, on the next task, the next place, or the next job, we can often be primed and loaded, ready to go off at a moment's notice. Living ahead of ourselves is about more than missing the roses. We put ourselves in danger because misfires can easily happen.

Remember when you were primed and ready to respond "the next time"? The next time she criticizes or he's late; the next time a clerk ignores you or an appointment is changed ... "Well, they'd better look out!" You're waiting, your blood pressure elevated, your nerves taut; you're crouching, expectant, ready to fire.

And, inevitably, the event you have prepared for happens. Bang! Off you go. A lot of damage can be caused, particularly if the outburst was a misfire. Misfires happen a lot. After all, it's hard to know the whole story, to understand the problem. More often than not, the situation is not exactly as you thought. But it's too late. The damage has been done. In such cases, we sink our own ship.

Interestingly, our expectations of good times can play tricks on our enjoyment of what actually happens. We can look forward to a fine evening, a beautiful weekend, a great party, a perfect wedding, or the holiday of a lifetime. We can see it all laid out flawlessly in our minds and hopes.

Well, "flawless" events are exceedingly rare and almost non-existent in human affairs. The weather and the ways people interact with each other are awfully unpredictable. The margin for error — problems, mistakes, misadventure, and even full-blown disaster — is pretty high.

"Why did they have to argue on my wedding day?"

"The rain has spoiled everything."

"Will this plane ever take off?"

Which is why, when you ask how things went, people list everything that went wrong and not what went well.

Living ahead of ourselves makes us vulnerable: less able to see, enjoy, and deal with the present. Considering the fact that the present is really all we have, that can be a tragic mistake.

Should we plan for the future? Of course we should. But we should live in the present; we should see the roses and watch how the rain runs down their leaves.

SORRY

Canadians have a reputation for being very polite, for saying please, thank you, excuse me, and sorry. We say sorry a lot.

We are quick to say sorry for every little error we make. We even say the word when someone bumps into us, steps on our toes, or calls our telephone number by mistake. We even say it when we have to complain about bad service or major problems. Visitors from away are surprised at how often we say sorry when it is perfectly obvious we haven't done anything to apologize for. Why accept blame when we've done nothing wrong? Well, it's a way we have worked out to smooth out the bumps of everyday life. It's a preemptive strike to defuse the possibility of conflict or confrontation.

It is a Canadian thing. It is okay with us if other people find our quickness to say sorry amusing. We do it because it works. It probably contributes to the fact that, in Canada, we have a less confrontational way of life than people living in many other places. I suspect we'd have a lot less road rage if our autos were equipped with a blinking green light we could put on to say "sorry!"

Of course, saying sorry is not always about being polite or avoiding confrontation. Saying sorry when you have done something wrong can be a major step in healing and rebuilding a relationship. Apologies help us to deal with life's inevitable blunders and conflicts.

However, some apologies fall on deaf ears and some reek of insincerity.

There's the quick sorry given by someone caught red-handed. You know their only regret is getting caught. Next time they'll take greater pains not to be found out.

And there is the reluctant sorry given simply to stop criticism and defuse the injured one's anger. Behind such an apology you can sense their conviction that the problem is not so much what they have done but society's silly moralistic attitudes and your lack of understanding, tolerance, or a sense of humour.

And what about the apologies you have heard over and over? Saying sorry loses its currency if people never learn from their mistakes and never cease doing the things that hurt.

Some people are pros at twisting things around to set themselves as the victim. "Look, I said I'm sorry. What else do you want?" Translated, this means: "Sure, I made a mistake. I'm not perfect, but you are worse than I am! The problem now is not that I keep on doing what I do. The problem is you have stopped forgiving me."

Saying sorry, like just about anything else in life, can be pretty muddled. We feel a valid apology should be accompanied by some recognition that the speaker's action was hurtful, damaged a relationship, spoiled the atmosphere, or caused collateral damage. We don't expect people to make a public apology, to don sackcloth and ashes; however, some signal that they understand how they caused pain helps a lot.

We also agree an apology should come with the intention to do better, to be more aware of others' feelings, and with a plan not to repeat actions that produce disruption and pain.

Sincere apologies, saying you are sorry and trying to do better, are essential ingredients in helping us produce and live in a civil society.

However, there is an enduring belief that there is a logical connection between an apology and forgiveness: that forgiveness is supposed to follow an apology like night follows day. No one has to forgive. You can be remorseful and reform your ways, but that doesn't turn forgiveness into a demand note to be called in for payment. Forgiveness is always a gift. Whenever it is given, at the first embarrassed attempt at an apology or after a long process of self-examination and reform, it is always a gift.

Thus, all the apologies and regrets that arise in life are not as important in healing as the gift of forgiveness.

So, in the end, it is only the injured, the victim, who can heal a broken relationship. Makes you think, doesn't it? Sorry to have to remind you of that.

SMART CASUAL

The invitation said Smart Casual. A friend said it's what you wear to the golf club. That wasn't helpful. The only times I go to golf clubs are on formal occasions: weddings, banquets, retirement parties, and the like.

Smart casual? Maybe it means you are not to turn up super casual, wearing blue jeans with strategically placed rips and an ancient out-of-shape T-shirt honouring a rock concert no one remembers, or in a low-cut blouse with a disconcerting décolletage.

As my wife will attest, unless I'm suitably restrained, I'll turn up anywhere in a jacket or a blazer and probably a tie. It's my definition of smart casual.

I'm comfortable that way, but it bothers some people. I've a standard response when people ask why I'm all "dressed up." I tell them, "If I was visiting the Queen, I'd dress up to show respect for her, even though I don't know her. So why wouldn't I do the same for people I know?" That reply is so unexpected and raises so many questions, they quickly drop the subject.

These reflections arose because of advice I came across for people who are to be interviewed for a job over the telephone. It suggested they dress "professionally" before the telephone interview because, "You will have a different demeanour if you are wearing pyjamas versus wearing clothes … Those things are reflected in the voice even when people can't see you."

Some reports say dress-down Fridays are less productive than days when employees are in business attire. I suppose dressing down that day makes many feel their weekend has already begun, so they slack off. One thing is clear: How you dress has an impact on how you act and feel.

This has been proven over the years. The first municipal police force in Europe was established in Paris. At first the officers, in plain clothes, were sent into the gritty streets of the city with orders to control crowds, stop brawls, and maintain order, It didn't take long for the authorities to discover they had made a mistake. People saw no reason to take orders from people who looked just like any other ruffian on the street. And, apparently, when a brawl was in progress, the incognito police officers were not highly motivated to impose order in the streets. They opted to watch rather than risk injury.

Things improved magnificently when the officers were issued uniforms. The citizens accepted their authority, and the police lost their ability to avoid trouble.

Clothes can speak about status, skills, belonging, and responsibility. Uniforms worn by the military, policemen, and firemen clearly advertise their role in society as people with special skills, training, and responsibilities. (I'm one of the people who wish nurses still wore distinctive outfits that clearly indicated their skills, role, and authority. It would eliminate a lot of confusion in hospitals and uplift the profession.)

Young people instinctively know that the way you dress is important and sends out messages. Students in schools without set uniforms devise their own uniforms to define who they are or would like to be: the preppies, jocks, nerds, artists, toughs, goths, and princesses. Teens know clothes can be an expression of who you are or be a mask to hide behind. It can be fun to dress up or down.

However, creating an image has an influence on our inner being. Remember the advice about what you wear affecting the impression you give over the telephone?

It is strange how what we wear is not only about how we appear but also about how we feel about ourselves and how we act. That's why dress rehearsals are important in the theatre, the time when the actors don their Roman togas or trappings of royalty. At that moment, the actors take on the character they are to play. It is said that, when the actor George C. Scott put on the uniform of General Patton, he became just like the tough, arrogant general.

What we wear is a message. Clothes talk for us and to us as they project a particular image. One could write a book on how clothes define people, communities, and groups.

What is clear in all this is that we need to see how what we wear can affect who we are and what we want to become.

Maybe I should stop wearing ties when invitations say Smart Casual.

OOPS!

I lay on a gurney waiting to have an angiogram at the hospital. My feet stuck out from under the skimpy sheet. An intern came by, checked my right foot, and marked an X on it.

I asked him what that was all about.

"I marked the pulse point just in case we need to check blood flow in your leg after we're done," he said.

Obviously this was a precaution based on experience. I'm glad they learn from experience. The one word you don't want your surgeon to utter is "oops!"

No one wants mistakes to happen, and yet mistakes, errors, and the odd "oops" are part of everyday life. Watch pros at work, craftspeople, doctors, and managers, and you'll notice they follow set routines. Hold the tool this way … slow down … always check that pressure gauge … be sure to rerun the calculations. Such instructions are clear evidence of mistakes made and learned from.

After Thomas Edison, the great inventor, had tried a thousand possible filaments for a light bulb, he was asked if he was frustrated by so many failures. Edison said he was not dismayed, for he now knew a thousand things that didn't work. In time, it took three thousand tries before his light bulb worked. Not many people have such a positive attitude to having failures and making mistakes.

I should have said "adults," not "people." You'll have noticed that babies learn to walk by falling down a lot, by a process of trial and error. That's how little children learn most things: Mistakes are a natural part of the process of learning.

That may be true, but the hard fact is that making mistakes is equated with failure. We expect that, if we are good, we'll get things right all the time.

It is difficult to grow up in our competitive culture without being embarrassed about making mistakes. A lot of us don't handle our goof-ups very well. So we develop strategies to deal with the possibilities of making mistakes. We work hard to be very careful and we try to avoid risks and new ventures lest we fumble the ball, make a mess, or get lost.

When we do make mistakes, we have defensive measures that kick into place: Sometimes we boldly imply it is all part of the plan, other times we defend our goof-proof image by claiming we had the wrong information, the wrong equipment, or not enough time, all of which leaves us with more fallback positions: We were overtired, or had a headache, not to mention the many variations of school-day excuses, such as "the dog ate my project."

Why do children, who joyfully learn to walk by falling down, turn into adults who have so much difficulty in dealing with mistakes, blunders, and the inevitable "oops"?

Early on, from parents, playmates, and teachers, we absorb a subtle message: Mistakes are bad; they are to be avoided: We must be careful or we will look foolish. We learn to laugh at people who make mistakes. It is all compounded by the way the education system works. Tests, with their emphasis on getting things 100 percent right, skew the learning process, which is mostly the process of learning from mistakes.

Wrong answers are not a sign of failure. They are a natural part of the learning process. Maybe we should feel sorry for those who get 100 percent. They are probably under-challenged and may not be gaining the skills they need to deal with mistakes. Edison knew that mistakes and errors, discovering what doesn't work — even falling down — are an essential part of the learning process.

To move ahead, there are a few things we can do. The first is to accept that, as long as we live, mistakes are bound to happen. We'll make them, and other people will make them. It is part of life; it's no big deal. If you are not making a few mistakes, you've probably stopped growing.

So we might as well set aside all our time-honoured strategies: avoiding risks, looking for someone or something to blame, and trying to maintain a "goof-proof" image. We need to let go of all our tired excuses. Feel free to have a new attitude, a new way of moving forward. All of life should be a time of learning and growing.

I'm working on it. With all the mistakes I make, it seems a good plan.

A TIME OF TRANSFORMATION

It will soon be time to watch Charles Dickens' story *A Christmas Carol* on television. It wouldn't seem like the holiday season without witnessing the story of Ebenezer Scrooge and Tiny Tim. Of all the actors who have played Scrooge over the years, none matches Alastair Sim.

To play Scrooge, you have to master three characters. One of them is easy to portray: Humbug Scrooge, the grumpy, grasping, greedy, ungrateful tormentor of his clerk Bob Cratchit. So is Haunted Scrooge, coping with the ghosts of Marley and of the past, present, and future. Getting Scrooge's fear and torment right is manageable territory for many actors. The real test is in playing the third character: Transformed Scrooge. That's where Sim excels. He captures the desire of the Scrooge who wakes up on Christmas morning to be a new person and make amends. Above all, he perfectly shows Scrooge's joy.

Some of you may remember the way Sim plays the scene in which Scrooge, sitting on the stairs with his servant, bubbles with joy, "I'm as light as a feather. I am as happy as an angel. I am as merry as a schoolboy. I am as giddy as a drunken man. A merry Christmas to everybody! A happy New Year to all the world!"

Transformation is the central message of Dickens' *A Christmas Carol*. Consequences arise from the way a life is lived. At Scrooge's neglected gravestone, the last spirit — the one who showed him the future his actions would create — says, "Men's courses will foreshadow certain ends, to which, if persevered in, they must lead. But if the courses be departed from, the ends will change."

"Say it is thus with what you show me!" Scrooge pleads.

The Spirit does not, and cannot, answer. What will be depends on Ebenezer Scrooge.

Sim understood the Transformed Scrooge of Christmas morning. He understood Scrooge wasn't just experiencing a fit of irrational exuberance. He was undergoing a profound change in his life. He was taking charge. He was going to make the law of consequences work for good, work for him.

Unlike many stories associated with Christmas, the change that takes place in Scrooge's life is not caused by some sort of magical intervention. The ghosts do not force Scrooge to change. Over the three nights of haunting, they simply set the facts before him. It is up to him to decide what to do and how to proceed. On Christmas morning, Scrooge is a man who had decided to change. It was not too late to change; an old scoundrel could live a new life.

As the past was determined by his actions, he needed to change the way he acted. Change does not come from deciding to stop being angry, irritable, impatient, or self-centred. Life is changed by displacing old actions with new ones.

Actor Alastair Sim perfectly captures the new Scrooge of Christmas morning. Scrooge springs into action. He is impressively cheerful, sends a goose to Bob Cratchit's house, smiles at people on the street, seeks out his nephew, and joins the Christmas celebrations. He immediately begins to be the person he desires to be.

Scrooge doesn't care if people laugh at him, if they suspect he has some dark ulterior motive or has lost his senses. As Charles Dickens writes, "... He was wise enough to know that [there is] nothing on this globe, for good, at which some people did not have their fill of laughter in the outset; knowing that such as these would be blind anyway, [Scrooge] thought it quite as well that they should wrinkle up their eyes in grins ... His own heart laughed: and that was quite enough for him."

Sim catches Scrooge's transformation from Humbug Scrooge, one who built his reputation and character by practicing meanness and contempt for the poor, to someone who — one act at a time, day after day, by the steady application of kindness, thanksgiving, and generosity — would build a new life and a new character.

Sim's Scrooge demonstrates why Dickens' *A Christmas Carol*, which is about hope, change, and transformation, is a classic story. Scrooge "... became as good a friend, as good a master, and as good a man, as the good old city knew, or any other good city, town, or borough, in the good old world."

Which naturally makes you wonder why so many people go through life being old humbugs.

PART THREE
RECOGNIZING LIFE'S GIFTS

"WHAT IF"

Recently there seem to be a lot of "what if" books and television programs coming out. What if the British had lost the air war over Kent? What if Presidents Abraham Lincoln or John F. Kennedy had not been assassinated? What if Napoleon's Grand Army had won the battle of Waterloo … if the Berlin Wall still stood … if Anwar Sadat, President of Egypt, had not flown to Tel Aviv to negotiate peace with Israel … if the Aztecs had defeated the Spanish adventurers?

"What if" stories are pure speculation. While many issues have been decided by the narrowest of margins — a bridge held or captured, a sudden storm throwing a fleet off course, the death of a leader, an assassination — the courses of action following the events are also important. The follow-up decisions, the opportunities taken advantage of, could be even more important. Writers of what if stories, if their plots are to have any element of credibility, need to invent a whole series of "what ifs" to navigate the turns and forks in the road and the many alternate paths and chancy events.

Also, while one often can put a finger on the moment when the tide turned — the storming of the Winter Palace in St. Petersburg, or Columbus' discovery of America — the changes that came to pass are often inevitable. Dramatic forces, sea-changes, were at work: the anger and poverty of the masses in Russia; the huge advances in ship design and navigation in the mid-fifteenth century. Thus, sooner or later, the same outcomes would have emerged. Add in the interplay of race, religion, economics, geography, technology, and shifts in climate, demographics, and migrations, and it is clear that forecasting what will happen, or "what might have happened if," becomes endlessly complex.

I'm not trying to put down the writers of these stories, nor am I trying to diminish the importance of the historic events — or the heroes — long recognized as the engines of change. After all, what this is all about is our lives.

Our lives? Yes, our lives often turn on an event, a decision taken, a chance encounter, a challenge met and overcome. Many paths and decisions have brought us to the present time to create who we are.

Much of our personal history is about the kind of family, the teachers, friends, and mentors we have had, the people who put a good word in our ear or spoke on our behalf. Our story is about having second chances, about when we were in the right place at the right time; it's like the credit card commercial says: "priceless."

We are also subject to the sea-changes around us: demographic shifts, wars, depressions, boom times, what generation you're in — baby boomer or Generation X — climate change, and the advance of technology. For example, on a Friday evening in the mid-1950s, a friend and his workmates celebrated the end of his apprenticeship as a lithographer. The next Monday morning, the company announced it was switching to modern photo-lithography. There is not much we can do to affect such realities.

All that does not stop us from wondering how things might have worked out if we'd made different decisions along the way. I've wondered how my life would've been if I'd taken my chance to apprentice as an architect. A little bit of this sort of nostalgia goes a long way. It wouldn't be good to be like a worn-out boxer lamenting, "I could've been the champ." Living with what *might* have been doesn't help us make decisions in the present. Thankfully, most of us get on with the life we have built.

However, working through the "what ifs" can be helpful, if we find there a sense of humility and gratitude.

The words of W. E. Henley — "I am the master of my fate: I am the captain of my soul" — are only partly true. While what we decide and do is obviously important, we are not self-made. It is humbling to remember how thin the line can be between success and failure, of how opportunities can appear from out of the blue, of how much we have been helped by the contributions of others, by the foundations they built, and the words of encouragement they gave us when we needed a boost. That's where gratitude comes in.

To thank someone who helped us, to pass on the blessing by helping someone else, is a sure sign that we have a grasp of what life is all about. A measure of humility and gratitude. Now *that's* a good thing.

BUSY, BUSY, BUSY

"I'm busy on the twelfth. What about the nineteenth?"

"Not good, I'll be flying back from Calgary that morning."

"Okay, how's the twenty-third?"

The pages of daytimers and screens of smartphones snapped and flashed as four people in the hall tried to arrange a meeting. As they negotiated, they stole quick glances at each other's calendars and squeezed in their complaints about how busy they were.

You would have thought the complainers were secretly proud of how full their schedules were, that it was all a contest, a game. The one with the fullest schedule wins.

We're busy and we're proud of it.

The people who developed clocks some six hundred years ago would be amazed how clocks and calendars have taken over our lives, how we parcel out our time in such small pieces. All they wanted to do was make sure the monks gathered to pray at the fixed hours. They would never understand how we worry about time: about wasting time by using too many key strokes on our computers, how impatient we can be waiting for a microwave oven to defrost and cook our dinner, or for a traffic light to change.

We are busy people. Most of us feel we need to book, schedule, organize, and fill our time outside work. We like to have an interesting program to talk about when we are asked, "So what are you doing this weekend?" When we have no exciting plans, a lot of us skillfully leave the impression that the only problem we have for the weekend is to fit everything in. To let people know we have nothing planned — that our Friday evening, or our weekend, is "empty" — would be an embarrassing sign of social incompetence.

We have bought the pop-psychology idea that all we have to fill every minute with some identifiable activity or some interesting project lest our time, our lives, will be wasted and empty and we will be a disgrace. We make plans with grim determination to save our time, our moments, from being empty. To us, time is like a vessel to be filled.

This idea is nonsense! There is always more than "now." Busy or idle, our moments are never empty. Every moment comes loaded with our memories, with traces of the sights and sounds of the past. In every moment, we have with us the stories of what generations of people have thought and said, of how they dreamed and solved their problems. Time is not an empty vessel, for we also bring to every moment our dreams, our hopes, and our plans for the future.

Being busy, being in the loop all the time, keeping up with the latest information, the fads and trends can be fun, but it probably blocks our ability to cope, to grow, and to be creative. We need time to think things through and to apply to our lives what we have heard, and seen, and learned.

We happen to be human beings and not machines. Our minds work at a thoroughly human pace. Our thinking processes are complex, organic, limited, and slow. We need time to think, to sort things out; we need precious private moments to find our way through the ideas and the flood of information around us, to match what we know, see, and feel with what we value; we need time to make sense of our experiences.

There is no quick way to form an insight, to create a new idea, to figure out a problem or what needs to be done. There is no quick way to allay an anxiety or show you care.

We are slow. But there is a paradox. It is only when we slow down and "do nothing" that we are most human and most productive.

Here's the plan: Take your calendar, protect some time every week, and mark it with a secret code like PT/RT (Private Thinking/Restoration Time). When people sneak a look at your book they'll see your time is taken and probably will be impressed by how busy your schedule is.

It works. Best of all, it can be the most enjoyable and productive part of the week.

FILLING IN THE BLANKS

Halfway through the musical *Fiddler on the Roof,* which is set in a traditional Jewish village in Russia, Tevye, the long-suffering father of three daughters, asks his wife in song, "Golde, do you love me?"

At such a question, Golde assumes Tevye must be sick or something. "For twenty-five years, I've washed your clothes, cooked your meals, cleaned your house, given you children, milked the cow; after twenty-five years, why talk of love now?"

Tevye persists. Over and over he asks, "Do you love me?" until finally Golde says, "For twenty-five years I've lived with him, fought with him, starved with him, twenty-five years my bed is his — if that's not love what is?"

To that Tevye says, "Then you love me!"

"I suppose I do," Golde replies.

And Tevye responds, "And I suppose I love you."

The song ends as they sing, together, "It doesn't change a thing, but even so, after twenty-five years, it is nice to know."

It is a touching moment in the musical. However, the last

line strikes a false note. Acknowledging their love for each other did make a difference. That's why Tevye persisted in asking his wife, "Do you love me?" It was important to know.

We need to know if we are appreciated, cared for, loved, and recognized. Kind words are the food of our spirits. That is why we can say someone is starved of affection. We need each other; we need to feed each other's spirits.

You see, words constitute the most natural way we interact with others. Words are the lubricant of human encounter, the main vehicle through which we express feelings and explain ideas and experiences. We use words to build understanding and to comfort one another.

There is a firm supposition that primitive people, the cave dwellers of long ago, communicated through grunts and body language, by jumping up and down and pointing. This idea persists, even though every group of people we've discovered, whether on remote islands or deep in jungles, has had a complex language. It seems that having a rich language is a basic element in being human and is an essential ingredient of community.

Talking is important. And yet you'll hear people say, "It goes without saying." Which means there are things that should, by observation alone, be crystal clear, be easily understood, and not need a lot of words and explanations. (Though you have probably noticed that the words "it goes without saying" are often the prelude to a long, complicated explanation.)

There is not an awful lot that actually "goes without saying." In *Fiddler on the Roof,* the care that Golde took of Tevye and his home all those years was not enough. The question remained, "Do you love me?"

However, a lot is left unsaid by design or by accident. In the vacuum, assumptions are made to fill in the blanks. Sometimes what we think has been implied in the silence, in the lack of communication, is right on. More often than not, what we fill in those blanks is the product of our wishful thinking or of our worst fears.

And so we say, "But I thought that's what you wanted!" and "Where did you ever get that idea?" When hopes and fears fill the blanks, a lot can go wrong. It is the stuff of novels and plays, tragedies and comedies, and, sadly, of real life. All of us have been caught on both sides of the problem. With all the confusion in relationships, all the wrong assumptions swirling around us, we all should probably work at doing better.

Where to begin? One obvious area that suffers when we assume that "it goes without saying" is in showing gratitude and appreciation. Nothing can cause someone's spirit to dry up and shrivel more than the feeling that they're unappreciated.

In a world that is overly judgmental and critical, in an age where people seem to feel that they need to express every bit of anger and irritation, we all need to hear a lot of kind words. Tevye and Golde are certainly not the only people who have left such important things unsaid for such a long time.

Gratitude and appreciation: These are good places to start. Work on that for a while, and you'll undoubtedly find a lot more things that should never be left unsaid. It is not good to leave a lot of blanks to be filled in.

WHAT IT MEANS TO HAVE 20-20 HINDSIGHT

To paraphrase the philosopher Kierkegaard, we live life forward but understand it looking backward. Looking back, we all have 20-20 vision. Maybe it is the gang I hang out with, but I seem to hear a lot about the wrong turns and missed opportunities of life. "I could have bought that piece of land ... taken that chance ... changed my job then ... spent my time at school better ... exercised more ... never started smoking ... refused to run with the crowd. Then today my life would be so much better than it is now." Well, you know the litany.

When someone takes that sad trip down memory lane to revisit all the "might-have-beens," the standard advice from friends usually comes in three pieces.

The first: It is impossible to know what would have happened if you had taken that other path. There are too many unknowns. This is undoubtedly true.

The second: You should set the past aside and be grateful for what you have now. Stop beating yourself up. Be thankful. You've survived and done well enough. And besides, maybe fame and fortune are not all that grand, maybe they don't hold a guarantee of happiness either. This is good advice.

The third: Look to the future. The future is all we have to deal with, so put the past behind you. This is also good advice.

However, it seems that in all the talk about might-have-beens, one simple truth is revealed by our 20-20 hindsight: what could be called a law of consequences. When we complain about what might have been — about missing chances — we are talking about our personal experiences with the law of consequences. Looking back, we know it matters what we do or don't do. Hindsight tells us our choices matter, that our actions or lack of action produced consequences. In short, it matters what we do. This is one of life's most important lessons.

Now, we might want to live free and easy with the attitude that it really doesn't matter all that much what we do. Live it up, try this, forget that rule, it won't be noticed, we can fix it later, it's no big deal. "I'll be the master of my fate, the captain of my soul." Looking back, we know all that is garbage. It matters what is done and not done, for the law of consequences is real.

It is not a bad law, and it is not capricious. It delivers good and poor results according to what is done. The law of consequences applies to all we do, all the seeds we sow, all the choices we make. For the things that bring light, joy, and blessing to our lives are often consequences of the choices we made and the roads we have taken. Thus, the law allows us to see what went right: the things that worked and brought good results. So good choices bring good returns.

Which is, of course, the message of the classic 1946 movie

It's a Wonderful Life starring Jimmy Stewart and Donna Reed. It is about a character named George Bailey, who, facing bankruptcy, feels his life has been a complete failure, so he contemplates suicide. Clarence, an angel, arranges it so George can visit his town as if he had not lived. The movie dramatizes the consequences one life can have.

No one back then expected the movie to become a classic, but it is now an annual part of our Christmas TV fare. In one movie directory, it is dismissed as a "feel good" film. Is that ever a put-down! Well, as so often happens, the critics and the cynics have got it all wrong. It is a classic movie not because everything turns out well in the end and good triumphs but because it is honest; it deals with real life as it dramatizes the law of consequences.

So, good news: With all this 20-20 hindsight that we're all so richly blessed with, we know that what we do matters. Our lives matter in the scheme of things. There are consequences that are impartially reckoned. And so, each one of us has the power to mould the future. Actually, we are doing it all the time, for good or for ill.

To change things, all we have to do is apply our 20-20 vision forward and not backward.

ACCENTUATING THE POSITIVE

My guess is that collecting is the most widespread hobby there is. Ninety percent of us have collections, active or stashed away. (I made that statistic up, but it is probably low.)

One thing is clear, there are no rules about what one can or cannot collect. Anything goes: playing cards, postcards, hockey cards, stamps, golf balls, glass jars, salt shakers, thimbles, pens, stuffed rabbits, china pigs, old tractors, tools, coins, lapel pins, comic books, Lionel Trains, and "ancient" computers. Some may remember a report about a man, I believe from Saskatchewan, who collected old outhouses.

Of course, not every collector is serious. Serious is when you join collectors' clubs and travel to show-and-swap events. Most of us have modest collections — records by Elvis, china figurines, thimbles, spoons, regimental badges, that sort of stuff — but we're unlikely to drive miles out of our way to add to our collection. However, in our subconscious, we maintain an automatic alert system that draws our attention to opportunities to add to it. We are not out looking for anything, but in the confusion of events and images, we just "happen to see" what would fit into our collection. You weren't looking, but there it is. "Over there, in the corner. Can't you see it?"

What's really interesting is the way our minds can cut through the clutter and the noise around us to zero in on something without our specifically instructing it to do so. Every winter, we "reprogram" ourselves to watch out for ice when walking or driving. For a while, we need to concentrate, but, in time, being wary about ice becomes automatic.

Being able to program yourself is really neat. It may not be easy, but it can be done. Okay, you're probably wondering where all this is going. Just this: It seems apparent that a lot of us are unwittingly programmed to spot and remember the daily annoyances: the delays, the "idiot" at work, the number of red lights, the annoying drivers, the coffee that isn't piping hot, the stuff we have to redo.

It is amazing how many things can go wrong in a day, and it is easy for us to count them all up to produce the story of our day. This automatic search program pretty well concludes that, in the long run, we are hard used by life. We are prone to be cranky much of the time, because we have a lot of *those* days.

It is unlikely that this state of affairs is the result of a plan we've made at some point in our lives. It is hard to believe that many of us would have sat down and said to ourselves, "I'm going to count every little annoying thing; I plan to have a lot of *those* days." Things have just worked out this way. But is there anything we can do? Yes!

We can reprogram our default system. We do this all the

time, for example, to avoid falling on ice or skidding into the nearest ditch when winter arrives. To retrain ourselves each winter takes time, effort, and the odd bit of slipping and sliding, but we do it. After a few weeks, we are applying a different set of skills as we walk or drive. Why not retrain ourselves to modify which events we select to notice and react to instead of reinforcing this daily routine of accentuating the negative in our lives?

On the same days when things seem so wrong, we can get a different picture by resetting our system to look for and collect positive things: the driver who lets us change lanes, the people who made room for us on the elevator, the pleasant cashier, the task that went well, friendly greetings from strangers and friends, smiles and helping hands, and all the machines and gadgets that operate as they are supposed to.

It is not about filtering out reality; life *can* be tough. It is about modifying our alert system, about accentuating the positive. It's about navigating through the days, about not slipping, sliding, and crashing. It is having a new "default system" or, perhaps, having a new hobby: a way of seeing things that is less likely to make us discontented and cranky.

I've talked myself into it!

AN UNNATURAL CREATION

The year 2009 marked the two-hundredth anniversary of Charles Darwin's birth. It also was the hundred-and-fiftieth anniversary of the publication of his book *On the Origin of Species.* The book was a breakthrough, a brilliant explanation of how subtle biological changes in a species helped them adapt to their environment and prosper over time.

The process, called evolution, in which biological changes happen and the process of "natural selection" does its work, took over hundreds of thousands, even millions of years. The pace of biological change is infinitely slow.

Darwin's discoveries created a lot of excitement. They not only changed the way biology was taught and understood, but also inspired many — far outside the science of biology — to examine their core social, scientific, and religious ideas. Thus, Darwin's concepts of evolution and natural selection have been used as a key to understanding all kinds of scientific, social, and philosophical questions.

Darwin, however, claimed no expertise outside biology. He

was not a philosopher, political theorist, or theologian. He was aware that his discoveries did not even explain everything in biology.

After a hundred and fifty years, it is presumptuous to think much could be added to the debates that have raged for so long. But there is an issue of note that is not well understood. A few words may help.

While the major up-front conflict appears to be between Darwinians and Creationists, that debate is not the most important issue. Of greater importance is the way Darwin's biological theories have been used to explain how society works.

Early on, a group of theorists founded Social Darwinism, which promoted the idea that societies evolved by random selection in a process that was a mirror image of biological change. Herbert Spencer, one of the early members of the movement, coined the succulent phrase, "the survival of the fittest," which explains, in a nutshell, where Social Darwinists are coming from. Such ideas led, in time, to talk of master races, lesser breeds, and all sorts of evil.

Transferring theories from biology to society is fraught with danger. Biological change takes place over eons and eons of time, while the establishment of society — of culture — can be set pretty accurately as happening about five thousand years ago.

What caused this? Was there some genetic change in humanity? There's no evidence that humans have undergone any noticeable biological change for, well, eons. As a matter of fact, anthropologists and psychologists often claim we are ill-equipped to live in our crowded cities, in our fast-changing environment, with the same package of instincts, strengths, and weaknesses that served our ancestors as hunters and gatherers.

So what happened five thousand years ago that kick-started civilization? Writing was invented! Information could be recorded, passed on, packaged, and delivered across distances and across generations.

Society, civilization itself, is a human creation, not a natural process at all. It is the result of deliberate actions, hard lessons learned, skills shared, and knowledge passed on from generation to generation. We plot our own path and act against biological processes when we protect the vulnerable, the unfortunate, and the weak.

The historian Will Durant writes, "… Civilization is not something inborn or imperishable; it must be acquired anew by every generation … Man differs from the beast only by education … the technique of transmitting civilization."

Sadly, the history of society also records times of mayhem and barbarism when social order broke down. It is from hard lessons learned that authorities flood the streets with police officers when there is a power blackout.

There is nothing random about the growth of society; it is driven by what the author Margaret Visser calls "intentionality." In the short time since writing was invented, we have come a long way.

From all the generations before us who created civilization and culture, we have received a fantastic inheritance, one that comes with a solemn responsibility to preserve what is good and reach for what is better.

If that sounds sort of vague, I'm sorry. What it means is that we can't take civilization and culture for granted. We must, as members of the human race, be involved in the political process and in community life. We must resist the barbaric. For what we have built on Earth is unnatural and probably unique in the whole universe.

Our precarious creation needs our loving care.

IT'S BORING!

Sundays were different when I was young. Most businesses were closed, and nearly everyone had the day off. On Sundays, movie houses, fast-food outlets, and theatres were closed; nor were any professional baseball or hockey games scheduled. Even the T. Eaton Co. drew heavy drapes to cover its window displays. All that, of course, makes those Sundays sound terribly boring.

However, looking back to those years, the days I remember best are the Sundays. They were easy days when we visited family and friends. Days when I walked downtown with my father to buy a newspaper, when we canoed on the river, built snow forts all day, or talked with friends about everything and nothing. There was time to read on the porch or to lie on the grass and find lions, ships, and faces in the drifting clouds.

Sunday was a day for simply wandering about exploring the neighbourhood and the city parks. Boring? No, not really. They were calm, easy days with a different texture, character, and purpose.

When people first used the word "bored," they meant they

felt as if someone was boring a hole in their head: something like a migraine headache, I suspect. Later, perhaps as a result of the Industrial Revolution, the word came in handy to describe how it felt to do repetitive work, hour after hour, day in and day out.

Recently the meaning has opened up to encompass any sort of downtime, any lack of excitement or movement, anytime when we're not involved or entertained.

Boredom is a big issue these days. The entertainment industry has become expert at dashing from one dramatic event to another, delivering a jolt every minute or so to keep us riveted to the screen. Designers of clothes, buildings, automobiles, workplaces, and public spaces drive themselves to produce exciting new designs.

Excitement is in. That's probably why so many commercials feature people highly excited, even in ecstasy, over a new duster, a shampoo, or the new wall colour for the season.

These days, the ultimate put-down is to declare that something or someone is boring. Listening to the stars and celebrities on the late night talk shows, it appears the only unforgivable sin is to be boring. ("Just spell my name correctly.")

Complaints about being bored involve many issues: laying blame (Why did you drag me to this place?); demands for immediate action (Let's get out of here right away); and even making a less than subtle threat (If we stick around here, I'll be miserable and difficult … You'll be sorry). A lot of anger is included in being bored.

Margaret Visser, in CBC Radio's 2002 Massey Lectures, pointed out our society's prescription for boredom. "Bored is the motivating force of the consumer society. Bored people buy stuff for relief from their condition … Let me offer you a new car, a pair of shoes, a cruise. Distract yourself: You'll forget about your boredom for a while …"

Typically, it's a very short while. Curious people, as a teacher told us, are seldom bored for usually there is something of interest to observe, examine, or ponder.

Buying stuff, keeping busy, or being curious can't eliminate repetitive work, waiting times, or public speakers who drone on tediously. But maybe we can do something about the anger. That's what saps our strength, raises our blood pressure, and produces excessive tension and anxiety.

Somehow we manage to see doing repetitive work, being delayed — the boring things of life — as challenges to our self-worth, our dignity. Of course, this is not logical. Yet, it's easy to feel the delayed aircraft, the dull meeting, or the empty weekend as a personal affront. Anger is a way to fight back, to defend ourselves.

But anger is probably one of the least effective ways to deal with a boring situation and probably makes things worse.

Which brings us back to those Sundays long ago. Why weren't they boring? It was a matter of attitude. You couldn't take the nature of the day personally. It was not about you; it was the same for everyone. So you lived with the day, and, if you were lucky, you saw it is a gift, a day of rest and recharging, of discovery.

How can we live with "boring"? Simple, remember that it is not about you. Sometimes things are boring, sometimes not. That's the way life is. It is not about you.

LET IT HEAL

A woman told her story at the group-therapy session. Her eyes darkened and her cheeks flushed with anger as she recounted every detail of injustice, insult, pain, and injury. When she finished her story, words of support flowed toward her. "You poor thing" … "I understand how you feel." One woman crossed the room and gave her a warm, comforting hug. Grateful tears flowed down the woman's cheeks as waves of compassion filled the room. The counsellors were pleased; here was a perfect example of how therapy groups do their work.

A woman at the far end of the long couch asked, "How long ago did all this happen?"

Through the tears came this reply: "Eight-and-a-half years ago last week!"

The waves of compassion quickly receded. The room became very quiet as people thought she ought to have moved on and taken charge of her life by now. They sensed she would probably never heal the wounds she had allowed to fester. In the end, for the group, there was a positive outcome. When the session broke up, many had recommitted themselves to healing; no one wanted to carry their grief and anger for as long as that woman.

In ancient times, Darius the Great was king of the Persian empire, which reached from the east coast of the Mediterranean all the way to India. I've written about Darius before, about the day when he received a report that a group of freebooters, from a Greek city called Athens, had attacked and captured Sardis, a small city on the Mediterranean coast. You'll remember that Darius had never heard of Athens, so he asked his advisors to check. They reported that Athens was a small, independent Greek city-state in Attica. Darius was furious. How dare they attack a piece of his kingdom?

He could have ignored the incident, or ordered the governor of the province, where Sardis was located, to raise a force to remove the occupiers, or seek revenge on the Athenians he had just learned about. He took the last alternative.

Now, being king of a big empire was hard work. He knew that, with all the problems and initiatives brought before him, it would be easy to forget his intention to punish these bothersome Athenians. So he had a simple plan. To keep his anger fresh and to avoid forgetting his resolve to rectify the insult, he instructed his personal servant to say to him three times before presenting him with a meal, "Master, remember the Athenians." And thus, day after day, with every meal, Darius kept his anger alive. And his anger led to a long series of wars, to great battles on land and sea, to terrible defeats, magnificent victories, and huge loss of life.

I'm sure it is not so, but it seems to me that when I was a little squirt I was forever skinning my knees and elbows, always getting banged up and bandaged. One thing is for certain. My mother told me, over and over, "Don't pick at the scab! You'll only make it worse. Stop, or it won't heal." Of course she was right.

Sadly, the roots of a lot of the personal troubles we have, the dysfunctional relationships, arise because we relive our anger; we pick at our wounds, keeping them open and unhealed. Thus we are handicapped in dealing with the present in our status as victims. Keep picking and it won't heal.

A lot of leaders and communities follow Darius' tactics. The wars in the Balkans were about insults and injuries festering for generations; much of the sectarian bloodshed in the Middle East is rooted in events that took place thirteen hundred years ago. A Palestinian, commenting on the prospects for peace in his homeland, said maybe it'll come in the next generation. Not likely! Not as long as this generation, on all sides of the conflict, continues to pick away at the old wounds.

Sure, it is hard to walk away, to forgive and get on with your life, to resist the opportunities for revenge, and to bring civility into relationships. It is hard to go to an ancient enemy and call for healing and a new beginning.

But it seems the only way forward. That is, unless someone has a better suggestion.

THE STOREHOUSE

The year my sister had her appendix out, my leg was broken. (Notice the care I took in phrasing that bit about my leg. It wasn't my fault.) Back then, to get your appendix out was to be initiated into an in-group that discussed pain and operations and compared surgeons and scars. There was no group for kid brothers with broken legs.

An appendix is more interesting than a broken leg. Perhaps because the little squiggly appendage had no known purpose in our digestive system. Like nipples on men's chests, it was something left over in the evolutionary process, and so, in time, it shrank and nearly disappeared.

The proof of this theory was clear. Those who had their appendix removed seemed to get along quite well without it. And, as it could become seriously infected, doctors felt it might as well be removed. That's all good, I guess. I'm sure my sister has never missed her appendix. But, on the other hand, it seemed strange to me that we would have a useless organ in our bodies when everything else has a role in our survival.

As it turns out, a research team at Duke University Medical School has discovered that our much-maligned appendix has an honourable function in our digestive systems. The appendix is a storehouse for the good bacteria we need in our intestines to process the food we eat. Its job is to replenish our supply of bacteria if we suffer from serious diseases, like dysentery or cholera, that can remove all our good bacteria. The appendix's job is to insert the needed bacteria back into the system so we can process food. So the appendix is not useless. Imagine that!

The value of the appendix made me think of other things many have decided are not important, such as communities and neighbourhoods. With most Canadians living in cities and suburbs, the evidence is that most of us live pretty much among strangers. We may know our next-door neighbour, or someone down the hall, but we would be hard-pressed to recite the names of people across the street or around the corner.

The style these days is live and let live. We love our high fences and hedges, our patios at the back of the house, and our garage door openers that allow us to come and go without being delayed by chit-chat with neighbours. In our town, many new houses have been built with lovely Victorian verandas — all spindles and scrollwork. However, I have yet to spot anyone sitting on them, let alone waving from them at passersby.

Our lives are complex. What with our work and chores, we're too busy, too burdened, to give time to be involved in community stuff. We leave it to people who like that sort of activity and have lots of time on their hands; it's like having a hobby.

Communities were useful in the past, in rural areas and

towns where the pace was slow and everyone knew everyone, but we've moved away from all that. Now we're into "virtual communities." We go "face to face" in fleeting and shifting networks of people with mutual interests.

And so it is, when there is a tragedy on a street, a community, or a housing complex — a fire, a serious accident, an act of violence — reporters and police have a hard time finding anyone who knows anything about the people directly involved in the event. "I've seen them come and go … They've lived there for four or five years … seemed to be nice people … No, I don't know if they have any children … It is a shame what has happened …"

The community is like our appendix: It is a storehouse of resources. When there is an ice storm or a flood, when power is off, if crime seeps in, or someone is burned out, we suddenly discover how important communities can be. Working communities can save the day as people help one another by sharing skills and strengths so all get through the crisis.

PANDORA'S BOX

The ancient Greeks had myths to explain every twist and turn of the human condition: why some people succeeded and others didn't, why there is evil, that sort of thing.

One of the foundation myths recalls that the gods gave Pandora a box packed with evils that, if released, would plague humanity with sickness, vice, passions, greed, envy, and pride.

Pandora's task was to guard the box, to keep it shut so the evils would not break out to torment humanity. If they ever escaped, they could never be put back in. Well, through her carelessness, the box was opened, and out flew the evils. However, one evil was kept from escaping. The evil that remained trapped in the box was hope!

To the ancient Greeks, hope belonged on the list of evils. Hope was a curse. Their basic understanding was that the course of one's life, the movement of history, what is and shall be was determined by fate, by the fickle power of the ancient gods, not by our actions.

The powerful gods lived without rules, morality, or discernible plans, even though their actions determined outcomes on Earth. In Homer's *Iliad*, a story about the siege of Troy — you may remember the Trojan horse, Achilles, Hector, Agamemnon, Paris, and Helen of Troy — the outcome of every event, who won or lost, was determined by the gods working out their agendas and vanities.

With that belief, it is not surprising so many understood hope to be a curse, an evil. It was foolish to hope, for no one can challenge the power of the gods or fight against their own destiny.

Believing in fate, the ancients tried to placate the gods, whom they believed were open to flattery and bribery. They performed the required daily rituals, gave them gifts, made sacrifices, and went on pilgrimages to sacred places to honour them. When this activity had uncertain results, their fatalism led them to come up with philosophies to deal with despair.

Stoics trained themselves to expect nothing, hope for nothing, and accept whatever comes. Thus they would never be disappointed, hurt, or broken. Marcus Aurelius, a famous Stoic, wrote these words: "In all this murk and mire, in all this ceaseless flow of being and time, of changes imposed and changes endured, I can think of nothing that is worth prizing highly or pursuing seriously."

At the other philosophical extreme, the hedonists developed the policy of ignoring the world and all its troubles and concentrating as much as possible on personal pleasure: to eat, drink, and be merry. Their attitude was, if nothing we can do really matters, let's party.

Today, stoicism and hedonism are found everywhere one looks. Hope doesn't get much press.

We are fed on a view of the future that is unrelentingly grim: The course of our lives is set by our genes; we will soon run out of food, gas, and oil; the rich elite always rule and the 99 percent will always be ground down; global warming will bring massive migrations, revolts, or genocide. The terrible list seems endless. Any talk of hope is dismissed as blind optimism.

During the 2008 election primaries in the United States, Barack Obama said, "… hope is not blind optimism; the nation was built on hope. Hope is that real thing inside us that insists, despite all evidence to the contrary, that something better awaits us if we have the courage to reach for it, and work for it, and fight for it."

The ancient Greeks and the modern pundits with their endless messages of despair and disaster have it all wrong. Hope is a great blessing: It is the oxygen of the human spirit. Hope has the power to rescue and restore, to rebuild and revitalize the lives of people and the course of history. Far too many people believe Doris Day was expressing an unchanging universal truth when she sang, "Que sera, sera. Whatever will be, will be. The future's not ours to see."

Those who build their lives on hope are the ones who beat the odds and build the future.

DOING THE MATH

"The traffic is horrible. I had to wait forever for a parking spot at the plaza. From the highway, all the way down here, every light was red. There are so many stupid drivers these days …"

Traffic is a major source of frustration, anger, and annoyance for all of us. Traffic reports are much like weather reports. We can't stop storms or traffic tie-ups, yet it's good to know about them, particularly when we're not involved.

So, day by day, we've got gridlock, being on call 24/7, e-mails, cell phones, annoying clerks or customers, and long waits at the doctor's office: lots of hassle. No wonder so many people are on edge. It's strange, though, that while a lot lose it, others seem to manage hassles more easily, more calmly.

On average, day in and day out, everyone probably ends up with about an equal share of red lights, stupid drivers, and blockages. Yet, anxiety and rage aren't equally distributed. Some people have their blood pressure hit the roof, while others maintain their equilibrium and are even laid-back.

Do these people have different genes? Perhaps their schedule is not as heavy. Maybe they are into medication that cools their jets. It's hard to believe that genes, schedules, or drugs explain why some handle anxiety well and others barely get through the day.

It is really a math problem. How you feel often depends on what you are counting.

Count the problems, catalogue the hurts, add up the frustrations, keep a list of incomplete dreams or trips to the doctor — well, the numbers soon add up to create an impressive record of hassles, disappointments, and annoyances. And that, naturally, makes us feel hard done by, convinced that the cards are stacked against us. Then we become wary.

The hurts and frustrations we have added up set us on guard, expecting the last straw, as in "the straw that broke the camel's back." Actually, we are impatient in waiting for the last straw; we store up anger, all prepared for that moment. When the last straw comes, as it always does (there's always another red light, irritating e-mail, traffic holdup, or difficult encounter), we just lose it — as we have planned.

Yes, it really is a math problem.

Studies conducted by universities in California and Florida found that people who keep count of the things they are grateful for are healthier than those who add up all the bad things that happen to them.

I suppose they used questionnaires, interviews, and observations to produce graphs and percentages, that sort of thing.

It's interesting how we need scientific proof before we'll believe anything. The researchers discovered that something as simple as being grateful for everyday blessings, like getting home safely, having a job, a doctor, or a place to lay your head each night, makes a huge difference. Adding them up is good math. Instead of looking for the next hurt, you add up the good things: the ones that turn up in surprising places and from unexpected people.

The professors studied healthy students as well as people with incurable diseases and found those who counted their blessings not only had a better attitude and better mental health, but also were physically healthier. They even slept longer and felt more refreshed in the morning.

All this by doing the right math — by counting blessings. It sounds too simple. Okay, it is a simple idea. It may take practice to become aware of the good things and a while to get a new outlook, but it's worth the effort.

So, when you are stuck in a huge traffic crawl, don't see it as the last straw. Use the time to review the good stuff: family, home, job, health, friends, and tasks successfully accomplished.

You can see the traffic problem as a gift, a quiet time in a comfortable, climate controlled place with lovely music available at the touch of finger and a telephone to let people know you'll be late.

Count your blessings; see how it lowers your tension and blood pressure. Imagine being healthier by doing a different kind of math. It is certainly worth a try. I'm working on it. So far, so good.

WE'RE ALL PEACEMAKERS

It looks as if the habit of calling Toronto a world-class city is fading. The new way is to call it the fifth largest city in North America, after Mexico City, New York, Los Angeles, and Chicago. (Have you noticed that some TV news reports avoid calling Toronto by name and use the phrase "Canada's largest city"?)

Living in or around a big city is not the environment most of us grew up in. Many of us came from small communities. Even if you did grow up here, the city has grown up around you.

Small villages and towns outside the city one day found themselves becoming part of the GTA, the Greater Toronto Area. As I recall, nobody consulted the residents to see if that was all right with them. It just happened.

World class, fifth largest, GTA, mega-city: Whatever it is called, it means lots of people and many challenges. To live here is to cope with lots of strangers, heavy traffic, congestion, and high-rise living. Sadly, for many, living in a big city also equates to living in the midst of danger.

The media keep themselves busy giving us detailed reports of violence in the big city, describing home invasions, guns, drugs, road rage, and gang turf wars. Some reporters sum up city life as living on the "mean streets."

Every new outrage brings out calls for more police, tougher laws, and harsher penalties. The popular myth is that city living is dangerous, that it is a jungle out there, dog-eat-dog — an endless struggle for survival. It's a bad place to live if you want a peaceful life.

But people who have never lived in a large metropolitan city will be amazed to learn that living civilized, peaceful lives together is what we do.

We work at keeping the peace every day, and it works out pretty well. Steven Jay Gould, a Harvard biologist and an essayist, writes, "Homo sapiens is a remarkable genial species ... think of how many millions of hours we can log for most people on most days without noting anything more threatening than a raised third finger once a week or so."

We are skilled at defusing situations: We choose calm words, we walk away, we "let cooler heads prevail," we work hard to put people at ease. When we meet strangers, we comment on the weather, the traffic, the hockey team, insignificant chatter that has a serious purpose. It is a way of putting each other at ease, a way of showing acceptance and demonstrating that we are not a threat to one another. We are basically peacemakers.

And so, millions of us go about our lives peacefully every day in the big city and sleep soundly at night. And most of us have had no direct contact with anyone who has been a perpetrator or victim of violence, of robbery, or of road rage. Our lives are happily dull. And, to top it off, we don't have to be extra alert or super street-smart to live here. It is all because the vast majority of people we see day by day are also skilled peacemakers.

That's not news, but it is the truth. It's why the fifth largest city in North America is a livable, peaceful place. It is not because we have lots of police, courts, and security guards to protect us from the bad apples, nor is it because we have enlightened politicians and creative social programs, as important as they are in maintaining our community life. It is much simpler than that. We live together comfortably because the vast majority of ordinary people naturally work at peacemaking, at defusing possible confrontations.

Governments, police departments, and our structures and laws are working at their best when they are designed and dedicated to enhance and support the peacemaking skills that come naturally to all people.

We should always remember that the basic desire of all the people and communities within the complex urban community that is our city is to live in peace and harmony. This desire is the greatest resource we have to build communities on.

So to all, thanks. Thanks for being a peacemaker, thanks for all you do to help us all to live, work, and enjoy the amenities of city life in peace and harmony. It all matters, it all counts. Thanks.

PEACE IS A WIDE WORD

The CDs the kids are playing in the house are loud. The beeps from the computer games are annoying. "Can I have a little peace in here?" With such words, many parents plead for respite from the noise, for a little bit of quiet.

Peace, when you think about it, is a precious commodity. How nice it is to find it at the lake in the summer — to be "at peace with ourselves" or to have "peace of mind." Peace comes after a conflict is resolved. Sadly, for many, to have peace means guns and bombs will cease. Peace is a wide word that covers a lot of concepts and conditions.

With the War on Terrorism still churning away, it is important to think about peace.

From what we can gather from the veterans of the two world wars, peace meant survival, a release from constant tension, and a time of unbelievable silence. Peace was enough; talk of winners and losers would come much later.

Peace is mostly defined not by what *is* but by what *is not* happening: The noise ends, the conflict is resolved, tension and stress go away, guns are silent, the terror and tumult are over. So peace is, basically, the absence of things: a negative state of existence.

And that's the problem.

Now, we in North America had that sort of peace.

Many pundits have been telling us that we were naïve to sit back and enjoy the peaceful times we had. This claim is the first step in an argument that ends in making *us* guilty for the acts of terrorism, an argument that implies that by enjoying the peace, we set ourselves up for trouble. The attacks, therefore, were justified.

The only response worthy of such a notion is, "Gimme a break." We don't think about or handle peace differently from any other people on Earth. We are not abnormally weird, self-ish, or self-centred. People are people wherever they live. And, all over the world, people understand peace mostly as a passive state, as the absence of conflict and war.

Have no doubt, to be done with destruction, with killing and persecution, and to be done with the anger and the shouting — these are blessings not to be discounted.

Our Canadian armed forces, involved in peacekeeping all over the world, have shown amazing skill in separating warring factions and creating spaces where peace can take hold. The spaces are important, because a lot of people need time to heal their wounds, to plant their crops, to build and rebuild, to enjoy each day and have the opportunity to dance, sing, and laugh.

Peace is great; we need more of it. That might sound like a silly point to make. But it isn't. All who live at peace in our world need to find ways to grow peace. Through history, the ending of a war usually meant that peace was the result. But in these days of economic interdependence, population growth, and the globalization of everything, the absence of conflict doesn't always mean peace.

Few generations have spent much time, wealth, or effort in waging peace; it's nothing like the amount dedicated to waging wars. That's why it's time to change the game plan.

We have reason to be a little optimistic. Many people and organizations have been working, some for over fifty years, at building peace on Earth. International charitable organizations and UN agencies, often underfunded and uncertain of the way ahead, have moved beyond emergencies and disasters to help many people to live at peace, through better education, medical systems, roads, drinking water, and economic opportunities. By trial and error, they have learned a lot about what does and doesn't work.

We're better at war. Yet, some of the accomplishments, like South Africa's Truth and Reconciliation Commission, are brilliant steps forward.

Every country has its war or defence department that plans strategies and uses public wealth to ensure "the peace of the realm." What we need for the future are peace departments that plan strategies to foster peace on Earth.

Is that a utopian dream? Not at all. Sooner or later it will happen. The future demands it. When? How? Who? I'll leave it to you to figure that one out.

WILL YOU FIT INTO THE FUTURE?

When the first railroad was built in China in 1876 (a ten-mile line between Shanghai and Woosung), the people protested. They said it offended and disturbed the spirit of the Earth. Having enjoyed generations of stability in their daily lives, they were not interested in change. Their opposition was effective. The government bought the railroad from its builders, closed it, and heaved its rolling stock into the sea.

This footnote to history reveals just how accustomed our generation is to having things change.

It's speeding up. Three hundred years ago, people could be sure their grandchildren would have the same sort of life they did. People a hundred years later expected their grandchildren would see changes but the pace of their lives would still be governed by traditional ways. At the beginning of the last century, by 1900, people knew life in the next generations would be quite different from their own, but they expected firm links with their time to remain. At the turn of our current century, no one who has lived through the changes of the last few decades expects life twenty or thirty years from now to be anything like ours.

Change has a host of cheerleaders who can hardly wait to have the latest gadget. Many thrive on being in touch, online, connected twenty-four hours a day, seven days a week. And, if the promoters are to be believed, we all want refrigerators that will order milk, and medicine cabinets that will remind us to take our medication.

However, all this rapid change comes at a cost.

A Cambridge professor predicts that, in the twenty-first century, everything that was familiar when a person grew up will be antiquated before their lives are over. We won't be able to rely on traditional ways to help us find our footing. We will become nostalgic for the days we once knew. The value of our hard-earned knowledge and skills will fade almost as soon as they are acquired. That's not a prediction. It has been happening for two or three decades.

What change does to ordinary people will be a major issue in the twenty-first century. If we become detached from the past, from our own past, how will we cope? What can be done?

Tossing our cell phones and computers into the sea will solve nothing. After all, even as the people of Shanghai heaved the railroad's rolling stock into the sea and celebrated their victory, plans were underway to build other railroads in China.

How will we make it through, day by day, when everything changes? The big picture is, well, too big. It's easy to get caught trying to figure out national and global priorities for the future. It is too easy to say, "They should do something."

It is the ordinary people who carry the burdens of the world's problems and cope with the fallout. We are the ones who end up feeling disconnected, rootless. There has to be something we can do for ourselves.

There is. For thousands of generations, through huge changes, individuals and families have found strength and stability in remembering their past.

These days, for many, our links to the past have become weak. A lot of us have little idea about our roots and the history of our families. We understand how this has happened. Our families dispersed; we have been busy adjusting to the new. But the stories that could strengthen us and make us laugh have slipped away. Without the stories of family struggles, disasters, and victories, our view of life is narrow.

Our family trees, garnered from ancient church books and registry offices, present questions that taunt us. Did great-great-grandfather fight with Wellington in the battle of Waterloo? How could our aunt travel alone from the old country to this part of Canada? How did they manage to survive their first Canadian winter? How did they face the hard years, the changes and challenges in their lives and generations? We need the answers.

Why? Not to satisfy some romantic ideal or to escape from reality but to see how we can survive when everything is shaken. We need a deeper sense of identity, a sense of proportion and dignity: basic equipment to carry with us into that unknown land called the future.

HAVING MORE THAN ENOUGH

Do they fit the commercials around TV news broadcasts or the news around the commercials? Are there more commercials than news? It seems like it sometimes. The way advertising dominates TV reflects advertising's powerful role in our culture.

Advertising, which started out by telling us where to find the things we needed and how one product is superior to another, has taken on the job of moulding our ideas about what we need, want, desire, and simply must have. Advertisers are in the business of creating wants, promoting lifestyles, and offering us solutions to problems we didn't know we had.

Is it any wonder a lot of us have long lists of dreams, ambitions, desires, wants, and unfulfilled expectations of life? It is not surprising so many feel unfortunate, abused, hard done by, and dissatisfied with their lives. The system is designed to create envy, which gives birth to the notion that, for some reason, the world is against us. A current automobile commercial plays on that sense of dissatisfaction when it asks if the good things in life are only for the rich.

An English historian writes, "The truth seems to be that … some millions of people have been aspiring to live as only a few hundred thousand of people could in fact afford to live."

While we strive to climb higher and pore over our list of wants and perceived needs, it is good to get a little perspective on the status of our material condition and of how we are doing.

Well, to start, the average person in Canada, living in a small house or apartment, has more luxuries than anyone in our country had a hundred years ago.

We have electricity, running water, flush toilets, and warm, dry places to sleep. We have clothes for the summer, better food, and access to medical care, and we enjoy longer lives. We live better than any medieval king in his damp, drafty castle and better than the first Queen Elizabeth, and without her problems. Queen Victoria's husband, Prince Albert, died of a disease easily cured today. I forgot to mention other things we have — CDs, TV movies, microwaves, refrigerators, and air travel — but you know all that.

As well, there are a lot of lovely things out there for us: new styles, designs, and so many places to go.

But do you remember the old adage about pessimists and optimists? A pessimist sees a glass as half empty, and an optimist sees the same glass as half full. I'm not sure where I am in that test. There are times when I'm a half-full type and there are times when I'm with the pessimists and worry about things being half empty.

I have figured one thing out, though. Often what determines how you feel is not so much whether your glass is half full or half empty but about the size of the container you are dealing with. Filling a glass is quite a different proposition from trying to fill a two-gallon pail or a steel drum.

Abundance means overflowing, plentifulness: having more than enough. Thus it doesn't depend on how much you have, but on the size of the container you are trying to fill.

I'm not trying to tell you that to be really content you need to have nothing and want nothing. Some great thinkers, like the ancient Greek, Diogenes, advocated that way of life and actually lived it. He lived in a tub he carried around. If everyone took his advice, there would be no one to make tubs.

What is important is to be aware of the subtle pressure on us day after day to work at filling huge containers and to see how our struggle — to buy and have and do — generates so much discontent and a sense that we have screwed up our lives.

It's that damn forty-five-gallon drum parked in the middle of our lives. We can start taking control by seeing ourselves as lugging one of these throughout our day. Roll it out the door, jam it into the car, carry it on the bus, bring it into the shopping centre, and park it by your desk at work. It becomes clear that life works better with smaller containers.

Abundance is really about having plenty with spare to share.

THE FRONT-LINE RAPID ACTION FORCE

Words crackle from the intercom in the foyer: "Who's there?"

"Keith from Meals on Wheels."

The door catch clicks to the words, "Come on up."

Maria's telephone rings. It is exactly ten in the morning. As she puts the receiver to her ear, she says, "Good morning, Alice …" It happens every day at ten. It means a lot when you're alone to have someone call to see how you are doing.

The youth group leader hurries to get into uniform and to the church hall before the thirty youngsters explode into the room.

At 7:30 in the evening, exactly twelve hours since he first checked his e-mail at the office, a man places a manila file marked "Group Home" on the table and says, as he passes out an agenda, "We have a lot of items to cover tonight."

"Who can be knocking at this hour?" a woman wonders as she pulls the front door open. "Well, come in, neighbour. Don't tell me it's time to donate to the Cancer Society again."

Volunteers come in all shapes and sizes. You find them in hospitals, schools, churches, clubs, community groups, and cultural societies, as well as serving in the far corners of the world. They raise money, run organizations, and provide hands-on, person-to-person help to so many. You'd need to do a lot of creative guessing to figure out how much time is given, how many people are helped, or how much money is raised by volunteers day after day.

The year 2001 was the Year of the Volunteer, twelve months when we were urged to recognize the contribution of volunteers to our communities. Maybe it is time for another year to recognize them.

Volunteers certainly deserve to be recognized for the work they do day after day, serving others, financing medical research, supporting cultural groups, leading teams … well, the list is almost endless.

But more to the point, volunteers and their organizations are our Front-line Rapid Action Force. Volunteers, reporting from the front lines, first identify the needs of our society long before they hit the radar screens of the news media or the politicians. By the time others catch up, volunteers are already working on the problems and involved in helping those who have fallen between the cracks. Long before homeless people made the news, volunteers were giving them warm clothes, sleeping bags, and hot soup.

Volunteers, and their organizations, are flexible and innovative. When floods, fires, and storms dislodge and disrupt people's lives, volunteers come together to help. When the job is done, they easily move on to other things. When problems arise, and no one is organized to deal with them, it is amazing to see how quickly volunteers show up to help and how quickly a new agency, committee, or society is created to make sure the work goes on.

And so it is, without a lot of fuss and bother, without a lot of rules, protocols, or complex procedures, that people are fed, clothed, and rescued. Using their energy, insights, experience, and compassion, volunteers get amazing things done. No wonder volunteers have a special place in our communities.

They are special because people know they do not have to do what they do. They have credibility because they give practical, down-to-earth help when and where it is needed, whether it is medicine, blankets, clean water, or comfort for the distressed. It is rapid, front-line, person-to-person, hands-on help.

Volunteers and their organizations often experiment, take risks, and test solutions that point the way for community and government programs. Volunteers are the innovators and the pathfinders in our society.

Of course, a lot of the help volunteers give is there for the long haul. A lot of it is imbued with a very special quality. In support groups, in twelve-step programs, help comes from men and women who can say, "I know. I've been there, done that. I've also struggled through the darkness." They know how to help in times of grief, of temptation, of loss. They know the power of kind words, of a helping hand given at the right moment when a little advice can be of benefit.

Volunteers are people who give themselves fully to life's adventures. They live on the front lines; they are our Rapid Reaction Force. It is not an exclusive club. Anyone can join. Everyone is welcome. Everyone can help.

TURNING PAGES

Erasmus, a famous scholar at the turn of the sixteenth century, was spooky. He read silently in a time when literate people read aloud or mumbled the words. The written words represented sounds, and to read was to recreate the sounds. Libraries were not quiet places. While other students were mumbling away, many wondered what Brother Erasmus was doing turning the pages of his books in silence.

Erasmus had a lot of pages to turn silently. By the time he was studying, printed books were plentiful and affordable. The printing presses, invented by Johannes Gutenberg just before Erasmus was born, had been churning out books all over Europe for thirty years. In those few years, hand-copied manuscripts became artifacts of a time past.

Today, many predict that, after six hundred years of dominance, paper books themselves will become artifacts of the past, replaced by electronic books. But the struggle between electronic and paper books has been going on longer than many expected. So far, printed books, to the amazement of most, have taken the first round. True, we're starting to see subway riders and vacationers reading electronic books, but so far predictions that the book as we know it is over have been premature.

Of course, printed books are convenient things. You don't need to learn new skills or buy expensive equipment to read them. Books are portable, they work in any environment, and they don't need to be plugged in or booted up. Books are equipped with handy tables of contents, indexes, and footnotes and they don't flicker or flash at you. Books, the end product of hundreds of years of testing and development, are sophisticated, elegant, and easy to use.

I'm sure there are more rounds to come. The struggle is not over. It may be, with the popularity of surfing the Internet and communicating by e-mail, that a totally new kind of publishing industry will arise to displace that built on the printing press.

It is hard to imagine the day when people will plan to curl up in a deep, overstuffed chair for an evening with a digital electronic text device. After all, who would want to run the risk of falling asleep and have your expensive electronic machine crash on the floor? I suspect people will be turning pages for a very long time to come.

One reason books have survived in the electronic revolution is that we like things of substance to be seen, touched, and held. Books have weight, and size, and are often beautiful objects in themselves. Flickering electronic texts are great for getting and organizing information, but things stored on a disc or memory chip seem temporary and insubstantial. They take no space, and they don't seem to belong anywhere, not really. They are "out there," "in there," "somewhere," but where? We like things we can touch.

A shelf of books is, in itself, a record of the passage of our lives. The books remind us of the road we have travelled, of the struggles we had to learn and understand, of discoveries we made, of people met in novels and ideas wrestled with in non-fiction.

That is why we find it so hard to discard books. Oh, some are easily given away, donated, or redeemed at second-hand bookstores, but so many are like friends. They are links to our past that remind us of what it was like then, what made us laugh and cry, what helped us to grow. They are friends who were patient as we went over and over paragraphs trying to grasp new ideas: friends waiting patiently by the chair to be picked up.

Books piled on shelves remind us of when we turned their pages on lazy summer days, cold winter nights, and long flights. It is hard to give away such friends, even if they have been unread and untouched for years. Besides, one day we might get around to reading them again.

You are right. I'm talking about an emotional attachment to books. And that's why I suspect that, a hundred years from now, people will be found everywhere sitting quietly, turning pages.

THE BEST MEDICINE

It is enough to make you laugh. There seems to be no end of silly things the experts will count and measure in all their surveys and polls. For example, did you catch the recent radio news item on laughter? European researchers did an extensive survey on the subject. Apparently, the average Italian laughs three times as much each day as a German does. The report said that some in Germany, embarrassed at being at the bottom of the "laughter poll," are joining laughter clubs to learn how to lighten up and take themselves less seriously. Now that's funny.

And yet, when you think about it, it sounds like a great idea. Most of us would do well to join a club like that.

It's fun to have a good laugh: the kind when your whole body gets involved in fall-down, tears-in-your-eyes, red-faced, uncontrollable laughter. A good laugh is a great tonic; it probably does more good for your body and your spiritual and mental health than anything else around. Remember the last time you had a great laugh? It felt good, didn't it? After, you probably said, "I needed that."

There is evidence that laughter is nature's way of releasing tension. It certainly gets the blood circulating, shakes up our spirits, and helps us to see things in new ways. People who study such things find evidence that those who laugh a lot manage their problems, pains, and losses more quickly and with less strain than those who don't.

We all enjoy laughing, yet a lot of us go through days when we don't laugh at all.

It's strange. Laughter is a basic, natural thing. Babies in their cribs, all by themselves, laugh for no apparent reason. Small children love to laugh and do so often. Sometimes all you need to do is to look at them to get a bout of laughter started. They laugh and laugh simply because it feels good.

We were all children once. We used to laugh a lot. We still love to laugh. So why don't we laugh more than we do? We seem to have trained ourselves not to laugh, to be serious, and to go about with long sour faces. Why?

You know how it goes. When you laugh, someone invariably asks, "What's so funny?" We're embarrassed because it's hard to give a reason. Laughter is an unreasonable, illogical, irrational activity. There doesn't need to be a reason to laugh. Why is laughter contagious? Why do people laugh because someone else laughs? The only reason is that laughing, by itself, makes them feel good. So when someone asks "What's so funny?" they laugh even more at such a silly question.

There is also the notion that you need a "good" sense of humour to laugh a lot and, if you have a "poor" sense of humour, you don't laugh much. But laughter has nothing to do with one's sense of humour. It is a natural phenomenon, part of the regular issue of human equipment. All jokes and comedians do is create a time when it is permissible to let our laughter out.

A lot of people are waiting to laugh when they're happy. They're holding back for a moment of true happiness so they can laugh. In this world, that's a hard moment to spot. You don't have to be happy to laugh. Actually, laughter can do a lot to make you happy.

Do you want to test this out? You'd probably want to try it alone at first. Start to laugh: Begin with "tee-hee," progress to "ha-ha," and in a few seconds real laughter kicks in, your diaphragm starts pumping air into your lungs, and your face gets red. You feel good, better, happier. It works.

At the end of a lecture in a huge classroom, the speaker invited us to laugh. "Fake it to make it," he said. He started, a few began to giggle, then in a minute or so the room was filled with laughter. We left the room laughing, relaxed, smiling. Passersby in the corridor asked, "What happened in there?"

"Nothing!" we said, and laughed some more.

No one is home. I'm going to test it out again.

Man that felt good. It is like a tonic. Mother Nature's best medicine. I've just got to laugh more. Maybe I'll start a laughter club.

HAPPY NEW YEAR, IT'S AUGUST 1!

I'll bet the astronomers, the philosophers, and the mathematicians thought they were pretty smart back then. I mean the characters who studied the movement of the stars, the rotation of the Earth around the sun, and decided our year had to begin on January 1.

They messed up. Bunch of nerds! I'm not talking about how they forgot to allow for leap year, that sort of thing. No. They had no idea how life works.

Who needs New Year's in January? It just doesn't pan out at all. No, wait a minute. It's probably just fine in New Zealand and Australia. While celebrating Christmas in the summer has to be weird, having New Year's then is perfect. It's living in the northern hemisphere that places New Year's in the wrong season of the year.

Midsummer. That's the right time to end a year and start a new one. In the summer, you have time to reflect on the past year, and leisure time to make plans for the future. It's the natural time to make a new start.

All those editors who assign young reporters each December to write articles about making New Year's resolutions waste a lot of paper and ink. Nobody makes meaningful resolutions in December. Except, perhaps, to swear off eggnog. Recently one of them confessed he had a hard time finding anyone who made resolutions.

Of course he had trouble. In the middle of winter, when we are in the midst of projects, hustling to get things done, and trying to survive the cold weather, no one has the time or the inclination to make resolutions. There are few leisure moments to think about the past or mull over lifestyle changes, career moves, or new beginnings.

That's summer stuff. Always has been, always will be. We northerners should have our New Year's Day on the first of August. That's when we are ready to think about making changes. We've had all of July — those wonderful long warm days at the lake, the lovely long evenings on the apartment balcony or strolling through the park, those idle hours appreciating the way the flowers grow and how bees gather honey — to review the past and to think about what went wrong and what went right since last summer.

So, by the first of August we're ready to sign up for courses, to push fixing the house to the top of the agenda; we're ready to get serious about an exercise program. Yep! The first of August we're ready to move on, to make changes, to start something new.

Circle August 1 on your calendar as your New Year's Day. Don't plan a party or anything like that. Leave all that noisy stuff back there with the Nerds' New Year. No, this is *your* New Year:

quiet, special, private, and personal. Work up to it slowly during July; don't rush things; see your New Year's Day as the beginning of an August-long process of beginning again. Ease into your plans; test out a few things; practice being different and doing things differently. By September, you will be on course.

Why bother? Well, before every one of us there is a multitude of doors and a host of things to know about, see, try, do, get involved in: things we will never stumble on, never "get around to" unless we resolve to do them. I don't mean expensive or exotic things. Just the things you sort of always wanted to do, your little dream. I'm sure most people, when they look back over their lives, don't express regret at having tried to do too many things. What most people regret is never having got around to doing the things they really would have enjoyed doing. They were forever "going to do it," but, without a plan, without resolutions, it never went from "going to do it" to accomplished fact.

New Year's, January 1, is a pain in the neck, but making resolutions, plans, and learning from the past — that's good stuff. Just do them on August 1, instead. It's a lot less complicated than heading for Australia.

HOW LITTLE THINGS CAN MEAN A LOT

I wonder who invented pockets. Someone did, you know. I never thought about things like pockets being invented until I saw a medieval tapestry hanging in the Victoria and Albert Museum in London, England. It showed a group of people on a pilgrimage, possibly to Canterbury. They had no pockets to put their stuff in. Instead they attached their stuff to leather thongs hanging down from their belts.

All around their waists all sorts of things dangled: purses, bags of food, cooking pots. It must have been quite a sight to see them trudge by with all their stuff swaying to and fro. I suppose it was in those times that thieves acquired the name "cut purses." In a crowd, a quick move with a sharp knife and a pilgrim's or a merchant's purse would be gone. Inventing pockets is not as big a thing as inventing an electric light or an airplane, but whoever invented pockets made life a lot simpler for people.

Then there is the business of shoes, of lefts and rights. Did you know that, for hundreds of years, shoe manufacturers used straight lasts? This meant that left and right shoes were identical.

No accommodation was made for the way feet are shaped. It must have been the origin of the idea that you had to break in your shoes. It was you or the shoes.

Originally I assumed that, like the pocket business, they did that a very long time ago. I checked with the Bata Shoe Museum in Toronto. They said it was in the 1860s, just 140 years ago, that most shoe manufacturers got around to making different shoes for left and right feet. There should be a monument for the person who had that simple idea and carried it out.

There are all sorts of things we take for granted, as givens: things that seem to have always been so. But someone had to figure out these "obvious" solutions. I wonder who first put handles on mugs and cups so we wouldn't burn our fingers holding hot drinks? And what about the person who figured out buttons? Before buttons, people either wrapped themselves in togas and saris, or struggled with laces and pins. And how about the fellow who invented matches? He sure made life a lot simpler for people. Before there were matches, you had to have a fire burning all the time, or be pretty good with flints and that sort of thing.

Today, already more than a decade into a new century, we seem to live in a time in which every problem is identified as being complicated and every solution as requiring some high-tech gadget: something to plug in or that comes with batteries included. And why is it that every personal problem has its own support group and therapist ready to schedule counselling sessions?

I'm not convinced everything is all that complicated. I'm for small solutions. Like using a simple Chinese fan in a warm room instead of a buzzing battery-driven one. Or like developing a new habit rather than getting into complicated programs.

A new habit? What do I mean? Well, let's say you're finding the days long and the normal daily problems and hassles a pain in the neck. What could you do? Well, you could decide to make a simple change in your life. Like being courteous and thankful all the time — to everyone. It is not complicated, not high-tech, but it can change the way your days go and the atmosphere you live in.

When you thank people for their help and service, for things often unnoticed, they are usually surprised and delighted. It is a way to give some measure of enjoyment to the day. After all, courtesy, expressing gratitude, is what lubricates our society. So it is good in itself.

Strangely there is a feedback loop in this. Your acts of courtesy, by themselves, add lightness to your day; they ease the strains and pressures. And, in the process, you find all sorts of things in your life to be thankful for, things you probably would have otherwise missed.

It is not on a par with inventing pockets, figuring out it takes different left and right shoes to make a pair, putting handles on mugs and buttons on clothes, or coming up with matches. But it is, like them, one of the small things that make living easier.

PREPARING FOR THE FUTURE

One of the first tasks that Britain's wartime Prime Minister, Winston Churchill, had in 1940 was to block a movement led by some parliamentarians to attack the leaders who hadn't heeded his pleas to rearm in order to counter Adolf Hitler's rise in power in Germany. He refused to let it happen.

"If the present tries to sit in judgment on the past, it will lose the future," he said.

The past has the power to cause us to "lose the future." I'm not referring to the claim that, if we do not learn from the past, we are destined to relive it. That is sort of true. Yet it assumes that we understand the complex forces at play in the past and foresee the outcome of what we do in the present.

Actually, we need to be reminded time after time that we live our lives in the midst of unexpected consequences. Which explains why, most of the time when we find we need to apologize, it's not for something we intended to happen but for an unexpected outcome.

For Churchill, meeting the future full-on required that the past, with all its dreariness and messiness, needed to be set aside. After the abuse and ridicule he endured in the pre-war years, it cannot have been an easy task. Yet it was essential in moving forward; there was a nation to be saved, a war to be won.

Getting mired in the past and losing the future is really easy. Life, after all, is not fair or easy. None of us gets by without having our ego knocked about by words said or implied. We need to be reminded over and over that the old adage, "Sticks and stones may break my bones, but names will never hurt me," is not true. The unfilled expectations, the injuries, the insults, the assaults, and the bullying can coalesce into black pools dragging us down and damaging the future before it arrives.

How we can we prepare for the future? There is a proven way to move ahead, a vital life skill that equips us to face the challenges life presents to every one of us: *to forgive.*

Okay, I know, that isn't the instinctive way most people deal with hurts, injuries, meanness, brutal attacks, and unrepentant enemies. The voice inside us screams ideas like "fight back, don't take it, get even, an eye for an eye, a tooth for a tooth," and, for many, a siren voice sings about the beauty of sweet revenge.

Of course, we all know that, in the end, our instincts betray us: The voice in us lies. Getting even and taking revenge will not put people in their places. Instead, such action invariably inspires people to mount a counterattack. Thus it is that family feuds, broken relationships, and unreasonable prejudices — and lots of other bad stuff — grow in rich soil. The present can be deeply stained by conflicts, injuries, and abuses that happened long ago.

For example, being born a Campbell or a MacDonald, you soon learn that these families were supposed to be traditional enemies. Why? Well, some of our Highland ancestors were grossly stupid over three hundred years ago. It's ridiculous, but not uncommon.

There seems to be no end to the list of ancient battles, insults, and prejudices that still demand to be set right before people can live on the same streets, cross each other's borders, or negotiate ways to move forward. Our instincts betray us, while forgiveness never does.

Okay. So, does forgiveness change the enemy? It might, or it might not. Should the wrongdoer apologize first? Not really, not often — actually, it is highly unlikely. Can I offer to forgive someone if there is remorse, a promise not to offend again? That's not forgiveness: It's like an episode of the game show *Let's Make a Deal*. Forgiveness is always a gift that only the injured can give.

By forgiving, *you* take charge of your life and how you feel; *they* lose the power to define who you are.

When you don't add fuel to the fire, the possibility exists for healing of renewed relationships. There's no guarantee that will happen — some people do not want to be forgiven because then they might lose power over you — but forgiving makes it a possibility.

The neat part of all this, the unexpected by-product, is that forgiveness brings peace into your life. Peace because you cease storing all the hurts and injuries in that deep, dark pool inside so that light penetrates where darkness once was. With that benefit, it's clear that forgiveness is not just part of an emergency kit; it's a way to live every day.

After all, no one wants to lose the future.

CPSIA information can be obtained at www.ICGtesting.com
Printed in the USA
LVOW101804280912

300783LV00005B/1/P